MUMMIES

THE WEIRD AND HORRIBLE LIBRARY

Other titles sure to chill and thrill you:

MONSTERS FROM THE MOVIES
by Thomas G. Aylesworth

POLTERGEISTS: HAUNTINGS AND THE HAUNTED
by David C. Knight

Scroll from The Book of the Dead

MUMMIES

Georgess McHargue

South Hunterdon Regional High School Library

J. B. LIPPINCOTT COMPANY
PHILADELPHIA AND NEW YORK

Copyright © 1972 by Georgess McHargue
All rights reserved
Printed in the United States of America
First edition

The author gratefully acknowledges permission to reproduce photographs from the following sources: The Metropolitan Museum of Art: pages 2, Gift of Edward S. Harkness, 1935; 35; 41, Gift of J. Pierpont Morgan, 1912; 45, Gift of Edward S. Harkness, 1917-18; 46, Museum Excavations 1919-1920/Edward S. Harkness and Rogers Fund, 1920; 48, The Carnarvaron Collection; 54, 58, 61, 64, 65, and 68, photographs by Harry Burton. The American Museum of Natural History: pages 19, 22, 31, 82, 85, 103, 109, 111, and 116. The photographs on pages 13, 40, 42, 43, 48, and 49 are reproduced from G. Elliot Smith's "The Royal Mummies," in *Catalogue Générale des Antiquités Egyptiennes du Musée du Caire*, Imprimerie de l'Institut Français d'Archaeologie Orientale, Cairo, 1912. Photographs on pages 25 (by N. Naumenkov) and 154 reproduced by permission of Tass from Sovfoto. Page 37, courtesy of The British Museum. Pages 39, 88, and 90, courtesy of the Smithsonian Institution. Photographs on pages 75-77 by Harold McCracken. Page 79, photo by E. S. Meany, from *Washington Magazine*, August 1906. Pages 92, 93, 94, 95, 97, 98, 99, and 101, from Reiss & Stubel, *The Necropolis of Ancón in Peru*, A. Asher, Berlin, 1880-87. Page 108, from the *Journal of the Polynesian Society*, vol. 26, 1917. Pages 141 and 146, BPC Publishing Limited. Pages 121-134, courtesy P. V. Glob, the National Museum of Denmark, Copenhagen.

U.S. Library of Congress Cataloging in Publication Data

McHargue, Georgess.
  Mummies.

  (The Weird and horrible library)
  SUMMARY: Discusses natural and embalmed mummies from the frozen mammoths of Siberia to shrunken heads in Ecuador.
  Bibliography: p.
  1. Mummies—Juvenile literature. [1. Mummies] I. Title.
  GT3340.M3   393'.3   72-2324
  ISBN-0-397-31281-4 (lib. bdg.)   ISBN-0-397-31417-5 (pbk.)

FOR BARBARA,

WHO ELSE?

CONTENTS

I	WHAT IS A MUMMY?	11
II	FROM MYTH TO MAMMOTH	18
III	ALL THE BEST EGYPTIANS	33
IV	THE YOUNG KING'S TREASURE	52
V	CHIEFTAINS AND HEADHUNTERS	72
VI	PEASANTS AND PALACE-DWELLERS	87
VII	ISLANDS AND OUTBACKS	105
VIII	BODIES IN THE BOGS	118
IX	CRYPTS, CRANKS, AND THE KREMLIN WALL	136
	SUGGESTIONS FOR FURTHER READING	155
	INDEX	156

Verily, . . . I have overthrown my enemies upon the earth, although my body lieth a mummy in the tomb.

>   Chapter LXXXVI, 13
>   The Papyrus of Ani
>   (The Book of the Dead)

I
What Is a Mummy?

A mummy is the body of an animal or a human being that has been preserved after death.

What does it mean to be preserved? The best way to understand is to know what happens to a body that is not preserved. Usually the flesh of a dead body decays quite rapidly. Bacteria in the air and soil go to work on the body, turning it back into the materials it was made of all along—a lot of water and some minerals. There are also enzymes inside the cells of the body itself that begin to make changes in the protein of the cells as soon as death occurs. These chemical changes are in general the same kind as those brought about by decay-producing bacteria—they turn the complicated protein molecules of living tissue into simpler molecules. Soon there is nothing left but the skeleton and eventually that also decays. It is lucky that this is so because if bodies did not decay they would be as bothersome to have around as old tin cans. Also, decayed bodies are turned back into fertile soil. Then new plants can grow and new animals can live on them.

Sometimes, however, a body does not decay in the usual way. If it is frozen or dried out or treated with some kinds of chemicals soon after death, the bacteria and enzymes cannot go to work on it or can only work very slowly. Then the body may be preserved for a very long time, even for centuries. It has become a mummy.

Some methods of mummification are generally referred to as *embalming*. Actually, the two words mean much the same thing. If a body has been successfully embalmed, we may say it is mummified. The only differences are that while some mummification is natural, embalming is always thought of as artificial. Sometimes embalming also refers particularly to the use of chemicals in preservation, rather than to such methods as drying and freezing. A natural mummy, the mummy of a person or animal that just happened to die when conditions were suitable for mummification, would certainly not be spoken of as embalmed.

Most mummies, the kind we think of first when we say the word mummy, are artificial. For thousands of years human beings have been mummifying human and animal bodies. Most people know that the ancient Egyptians were the greatest mummy-makers of all time. Every Egyptian hoped to have his body made into a mummy and by now hundreds of thousands of Egyptian mummies have been found. It is because one of the things the Egyptians did during mummification was to wrap the body in linen or cotton bandages that we usually think of mummies as lying on their backs and tightly wound with cloth. Or else, in horror movies, we expect them to be frightful, shrunken, bony figures trailing yards of wrapping.

Not all mummies are Egyptian, however. Mummies come from places all around the world, from Alaska to New Zealand and from the Canary Islands to Peru to Denmark. Some mummies are dried and some are frozen; some are lying down, some are sitting or kneeling, and others are standing up. They are found in pyramids, in caves, in cliff tombs, in bogs, in grass huts, in crypts, and even in churches. In fact, there are a great

Artificial mummy, Egypt

many different kinds of mummies and the only thing that is the same about them all is the way human beings seem to react to them.

Mummies are scary. Mummies are gruesome. Nevertheless, the mummy room of any museum is one of its most popular spots. Museum visitors from five to seventy-five often comment out loud as they gaze into the glass cases with the mummies inside.

"I'm not afraid!"
"Hey, lookit his face."
"Wow! Lemme out of here!"
"Very interesting."
"Hey, mister! Is that a real dead person?"
"Aw, I've seen lots worse things than that."

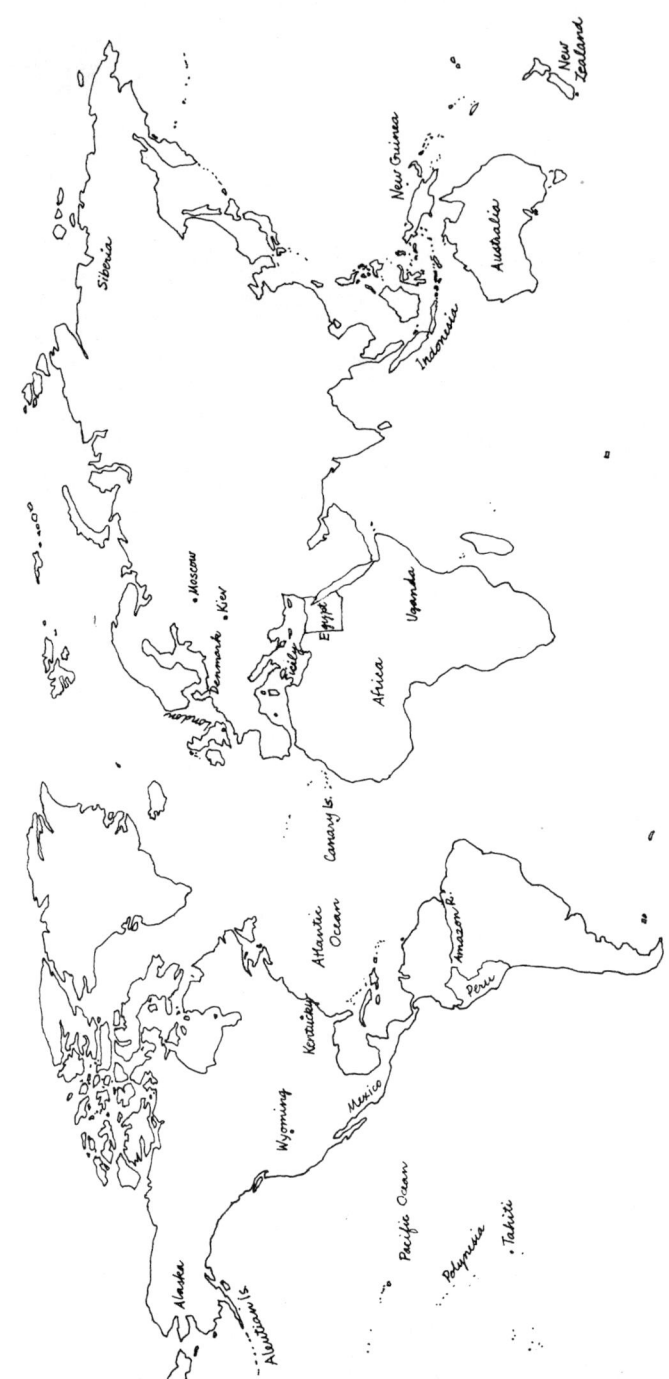

Mummies: principal places where they have been found

WHAT IS A MUMMY?

"Bet you wouldn't stay here alone at night for a million dollars."

"Yccch!"

Why is it that mummies arouse such feelings of curiosity, horror, and fascination? Perhaps it is for much the same reason that has led various groups of people in various times to make mummies in the first place. Mummies are dead bodies and human beings are afraid of death. That may sound like a pretty obvious statement. Yet it is amazing how hard we try to ignore the fact. If we bring up the subject of death, other people often act uncomfortable and change the subject. Nevertheless, it is very natural for the individual to wonder what death is and why we experience it. After all, it is the one thing that will certainly happen to everyone sooner or later. We want to ask such questions as: What is it like to die? Do people who are dead ever come alive again? Do we know when we are dead? What happens to us after we are dead? Do we still know what is going on in the world? If not, do we just disappear or do we find ourselves in another world we don't know anything about? And is that other world a better or a worse one than the one we are used to? Actually it is almost impossible for us to imagine what it would be like to be dead—but that fact will not keep us from trying.

We may be sure that in being curious about death we are no different from our earliest ancestors. The very first men, millions of years ago, must have asked themselves much the same questions as those we have just mentioned. They were afraid of dying because it seemed like the end of everything they had ever known before—the whole mixture of good and bad things we call life. And in wondering what came after death, they must have decided that the individual did not die completely. Instead, they thought that something called the soul or spirit went on living after the body had stopped moving and breathing. We know that our first forebears had ideas like this because in a few places we have found the graves they dug. Even the people known as Neanderthal men (the so-called cavemen), who disappeared from the earth at least twenty-five thousand years ago, dug graves of a special kind. They didn't just leave their dead for the wild animals to eat; they buried them carefully and *they buried various objects with them.* This is a very important fact because it shows that the Neanderthal people must have believed that the dead would have some *use* for the objects buried with them. The Neanderthals lived long before the invention of pottery or the discovery of metal, but they put such things as shells, chipped stone weapons, or bone necklaces into their graves. In their very simple way of life these objects were valuable. They certainly would not have been thrown away or carelessly dumped into the ground. The fact that they were placed there *on purpose* for the use of the spirit in the next world is the first example of the kind of idea about death that eventually led some people to make mummies. Once human beings began to believe that the spirit left the body after death, they began to wonder whether it might not some day come back to the body, or whether the welfare of the spirit might not depend on the welfare of the (presumably dead) body. From there, it is only a short step to the idea that the body must be preserved as well as possible, for the benefit of the departed spirit.

Of course the earliest mummies were probably natural. The people noticed that under certain special conditions the body did not decay in the ordinary way and then they tried to bring about the same result by all sorts of methods from magic formulas to herbs and chemicals. By trial and error they slowly learned what were the best ways of preventing decay, and then they had produced mummies.

Thus when human beings make mummies they are trying to give themselves a sort of immortality. That is, they are trying to show that death is not the end of everything and that

Natural mummies, found in Guanajuato, Mexico

there is some sort of life after death that involves the preserved body as well as the spirit.

There is nothing very horrifying about the idea of making mummies, once we understand the reason behind it. In fact, if we look carefully, there are many perfectly fascinating things to be learned from mummies, both the natural and the artificial kinds. Where else can we find out what the people of a certain age and place actually looked like, what they wore, how they did their hair, or even what diseases or injuries they died of and what they had for dinner beforehand?

In one case the discovery of the mummified remains of a huge extinct animal helped show that legends sometimes turn out to be based on fact and gave us an improved picture of what life was like on earth during the period of the last Ice Age, millions of years ago. Because the frozen mammoths are probably the oldest examples of mummies in the world, we will talk about them first.

II
From Myth to Mammoth

The oldest true mummies in the world are almost certainly to be found in the tundra regions of Siberia. There are two ways in which they are different from most of the other mummies we will talk about in this book. First of all, they are animals, woolly mammoths to be exact, while most other mummies are those of human beings. Second, there were centuries and centuries when no one knew there had ever been such creatures as mammoths at all—mummified or unmummified. Because they became extinct before there were any written records of their existence, we can know about them only from their remains. Unlike the dinosaurs, however, the mammoths left not only their bones but sometimes their entire carcasses for us to study.

The woolly mammoth was a species of elephant that roamed the northern parts of Europe, Asia, and North America between a million and half a million years ago. He was about nine or ten feet high at the shoulder, which though certainly large is not nearly as large as the imperial mammoth (13-1/2 feet) which lived on the plains of North America at the same period, or even as large as today's African elephant, who is

FROM MYTH TO MAMMOTH

often over twelve feet. Nevertheless, the woolly mammoth was a large beast, and his name has given us the adjective "mammoth," meaning anything that is especially huge. To protect himself against the bitter cold of the Ice Age, the woolly mammoth had a thick hide covered with long, woolly fur. He also carried a pair of very long, slender, curving tusks.

It was the mammoth's tusks that gave the world the first real clue to his existence. The peoples of ancient times were acquainted with the kinds of ivory that come from the tusks of the African and Indian elephants and from the teeth and tusks of whales and walruses. However, another kind of ivory sometimes appeared in the markets of China and, later, western Europe. This, although the buyers didn't know it, was mam-

An artistic reconstruction of the woolly mammoth (Elephas primigenius) *by Charles R. Knight*

moth ivory from Siberia. But although mammoth ivory was known outside Siberia as early as the fourth century B.C., the stories that were told to explain where it came from had to do with anything but mammoths.

The Chinese believed the source of the ivory from the north was a living beast they called the *Fyn shu*. It was described as a huge, slow animal with a long neck and a very small head, perhaps a misunderstanding of the mammoth's long trunk.

During the Middle Ages Arab traders occasionally brought mammoth tusks to Europe, where they were variously believed to be the claws of the Griffin, the horn of the Unicorn, or the teeth of the Dragon.

The first step on the road to finding out the real truth about the mammoths was taken by an English traveler named Josias Logan, who brought back with him from a visit to Russia in 1611 an enormous tooth. From that point on the quantity of mammoth ivory exported from Siberia grew steadily greater and the rumors about the nature of mammoths grew steadily wilder and more numerous. The Tartar people who lived in the area where the ivory was found believed the mammoth was a huge animal not unlike the Chinese Fyn shu. However, their version of the mammoth was said to live underground, to eat mud, to make great tunnels in the earth, and to die if ever it saw the light of day. The Tartars reported having found actual carcasses of the beasts frozen in the snow fields, and they, of course, were supposed to belong to those unlucky mammoths who had come out of their tunnels in daylight.

In 1692, the Russian czar Peter the Great sent a representative named Isbrant Ides to look into business opportunities in China. Since mammoth ivory was very valuable, the czar's representative was delighted to run across a man who claimed to bring out loads of it every year. The trader told Ides that he had once found an entire mammoth head in a section of frozen ground. The flesh had largely decayed but the bones were in excellent condition and (a vivid detail) still stained the color of blood.

The next report came in 1724, when another head and a large piece of hairy hide were found near the Indigirca River in the easternmost part of Siberia. In this case the finding of the skin was more important than that of the head because it was the first piece of evidence to show that the mammoths—even if they were elephants and not underground monsters—did not belong to either of the almost hairless species of elephant still living in India and Africa. This single hairy piece of hide indicated that a previously unknown species of elephant might have been able to survive the Siberian cold. It also put an end to a suggestion that had been made some years before, namely, that the mammoths had not been native to Siberia at all but had been African elephants who escaped from the famous invasion of Rome led by the African general Hannibal in 217 B.C. Hannibal had used elephants to help his army over the mountainous Alps north of Italy and someone eighteen hundred years later got the idea that those must be the same elephants that were turning up in Siberia. The only thing wrong with that notion was it would have required the elephants to wander at least 5,500 miles across some of the coldest, most mountainous country they could find instead of heading south toward places where they might find food and the sort of climate they were used to.

Thanks to reports from the Indigirca and other regions, the mammoth was scientifically recognized as a separate species in 1799, when the German anthropologist Johann Blumenbach gave it the Latin name of *Elephas primigenius*. At this time, however, the details of the mammoth's appearance and history could only be guessed at by scientists who were thousands of miles away.

Then, in 1801, a chief of the Siberian Tungus people

MUMMIES

named Ossip Schumakhof discovered near the mouth of the Lena River a frozen hummock of earth from which a huge tusk and part of an equally huge body had appeared after a recent thaw. Schumakhof was interested, but he was afraid to take any action. Among the Tungus it was believed that death or bad luck would visit anyone who touched the carcass of a mammoth. Schumakhof's first reaction, therefore, was to leave his discovery strictly alone. He kept to his decision for the next three years, only going back from time to time in order to see whether the huge carcass was still there. Each time he came, a little more of the big body had appeared from the thawing ground. In 1804 the valuable ivory tusks became too great a temptation for Schumakhof. He cut them off and traded them for goods of a considerable value, thus bringing the outside world the first news of the Lena River mammoth.

Two years later a well-known botanist named M. F. Adams

Frozen mammoth found on cliff in Siberia

was traveling through Russia and heard of Schumakhof's curious find. He started off for the Lena River immediately, only to discover on his arrival that the carcass had been damaged in a very startling way. Since no harm had come to Schumakhof after his removal of the tusks, the other Tungus men had lost their fear of it and, during the recent long, hard winter, had fed a large amount of the mammoth meat to their dogs! A scientist may expect all sorts of difficulties when he goes to inspect the remains of a creature that has been dead for twenty-five thousand years, but it can't be very often that he finds the beast has been partially eaten.

There is a lot of meat on a mammoth, however, and fortunately a good deal of the carcass was left for Adams to inspect. Adams took back with him to the museums of Europe a piece of hairy mammoth hide so heavy that it took ten men to lift it. This appears to have been the first actual sample of mammoth remains, aside from ivory, to have reached the outside world.

During the next century there were many further reports of frozen carcasses, but unfortunately no scientists were able to arrive on the scene before the finds had decayed or been otherwise destroyed. The idea of searching for mammoths had become so popular that there were even a few hoaxes on the subject—glowing reports of perfect carcasses that mysteriously disappeared just as the experts were about to arrive.

At last, in 1900, came the genuine find that everyone had been waiting for. On a cliff near the Beresovska River there occurred a small landslide which laid bare the carcass of a mammoth. Word of the event was brought by a Lamut tribesman who offered a tusk for sale in the nearest settlement. The trader who bought the tusk had the good sense to notify outside authorities and soon the Russian Academy of Sciences arranged to send an expedition to examine the find. The party was made up of a zoologist, a taxidermist, and a geologist, and the story of the difficulties the three men had in reaching the site where the mammoth had been found helps make it clear to us why mammoths had for so long been nothing but a local legend.

The mammoth had been discovered in August of 1900. It was June, 1901, before the party of investigators arrived in Yakutsk, the regional capital. Next they had to set out for the town of Sredne-Kolymsk, a journey of 1,500 miles almost straight north. There were no roads in the region and the only means of traveling over the thawing summer tundra was on foot or horseback with the baggage loaded onto pack animals. It took three months to reach Sredne-Kolymsk in this way. By then the geologist in the party was in a state of complete exhaustion and unable to go on. The head of the expedition, Dr. Otto Hertz, decided to take a local guide and travel the 200 miles that still lay between him and the mammoth, leaving the third member of the party to arrange transportation for whatever scientific specimens might be brought out. It was not until September of 1901, more than a year after the original discovery, that Hertz and his guide had their first sight of the Beresovska mammoth. But this time, Hertz soon realized, all their effort had not been wasted. The carcass had neither decayed nor been eaten by sledge dogs. It was easily the most complete and best preserved specimen of *Elephas primigenius* to have come to light so far.

The Beresovska mammoth was found in a sitting position, his hind legs stretched forward on the ground and his forelegs bent as if he were trying to rise. Except for the trunk and a little of the face, the carcass was almost exactly as it had been at the moment of death. The investigators could even see that there was still food between the animal's jaws and from the contents of the stomach they could tell what he had been feeding on before he met with his fatal accident. By the end of October, Hertz had finished digging out the carcass and had had the skeleton removed so that it could be taken back for

The Beresovska mammoth reassembled and displayed in the hall of the USSR Academy of Science's Zoological Museum in Leningrad

further study. At that time there were, of course, no electric freezers, so there was no way of preserving the entire mammoth once it had been removed from the permanent cold of Siberia. The expedition's dogs appeared delighted by the opportunity to eat a 25,000-year-old meal and Hertz was even a little tempted to try the meat himself. If only he had actually done so, we might have our first and only description of the taste of mummified mammoth.

Stripped of its meat, and therefore no longer a mummy, the mammoth skeleton was loaded on sledges and brought back in triumph to western Russia. It is now on display in the Zoological Museum of Leningrad, together with a reconstruction of the way the beast looked when it died.

This raises a very interesting question, one that may never be fully answered. How *did* the mammoths meet their end? What caused the death of a species that was apparently so numerous and successful? And why are mammoths the only Siberian mummies? After all, there is a huge area of frozen tundra in Siberia and other places. Why isn't the tundra dotted over with carcasses of other creatures, both ancient and modern?

The mystery appears to deepen when we consider the very large numbers of dead mammoths that are needed to account for the amount of mammoth ivory that has been found in Siberia alone. The best guess is that about fifty thousand tusks have been discovered over the years, and that would seem to mean that an astonishing number of mammoths died in such a way that their remains could later be found. What happened to them?

Probably the earliest suggestion to account for the death of the mammoths was that made by the followers of Baron Cuvier (1769–1832). Cuvier was one of the founding fathers of the science of geology and one of his principal ideas was that the world had been formed in a series of violent cataclysms such as the biblical Flood. According to Cuvier, whose views were widely accepted at the time when the first frozen mammoths were discovered, the mammoths and other extinct animals such as the dinosaurs had all been killed at once sometime before the creation of man.

The end of Cuvier's idea about the mammoths and also of that part of his theory came quite suddenly when the famous painted caves of France were first discovered. These caves contain pictures that were painted by some of the world's first men, the early hunters who lived by killing the game of Europe and Asia during the Ice Ages. These men painted pictures of the animals they hunted and among them are some very recognizable mammoths, woolly hair and all. Therefore, if the mammoths had lived at the same time as these early men, they had certainly not died in any worldwide disaster such as Cuvier had described.

Unfortunately, other ideas about the fate of the mammoths have often been equally unsatisfactory. Some writers on the subject believe that instead of dying before the early hunters, the mammoths were all killed off *by* them. Now, although it is certain that the human race has thoughtlessly caused the extinction of many species of animals in the course of history, it is hard to imagine how it could have done away with all of the mammoths. The hunters of the time had many other sources of food than the big woolly beasts with the long tusks. Horses, reindeer, wild cattle, antelopes, and many other animals were also plentiful and must have been easier to kill. Furthermore, as far as is known there simply were not enough men around to have brought the mammoth to extinction. The supply of mammoths was probably quite a lot larger than the demand for them as human food. And, interestingly enough, none of the frozen mammoths so far examined has shown signs of having been killed by men. For one thing, no wounds or weapons have been found. For another, one might suppose that if the mammoths had been killed without weapons, for example by being caught in pits or traps, they would duly have been eaten instead of being left to become frozen mummies.

Another suggestion has been that the mammoths all died of some disease, a fatal infection that simply dropped them in their tracks. This *could* be so, but there is just no evidence that it *is* so. The mammoths so far examined don't show any obvious signs of disease and until such signs are found, the idea of a fatal plague will have to be put down as a convenient but not very likely way out of the problem. The same proposal has often been made to explain the death of the dinosaurs, millions of years before the mammoths, and with just as little evidence.

If the mammoths didn't die of disease, they might have starved to death. The Ice Ages saw some very rapid changes of climate in various parts of the world, and it could be thought that the mammoths died when the weather became unfavorable for the growth of the plants they ate. However, the geological evidence is against this idea as well, since many mammoths have been found surrounded with evidence that the climate was much the same at the time of their death as it is now. Certainly the Siberian weather can never have been a great deal warmer, or the carcasses would have decayed long ago. Furthermore, several specimens, such as the Beresovska mammoth, have been found with their stomachs full of the same tender and edible native plants that still grow on the Siberian tundra in summer. This fact, of course, does not prove that starvation might not have affected the mammoth species as a whole, only that the few individual animals we are discussing were not starving at the time of their deaths. Perhaps they were only the lucky few. But the fact may make us wonder why only well-nourished, healthy mammoths seem to have become frozen.

One man, at least, has proposed a very spectacular answer to both the disappearance of the mammoths as a species and the amazingly good condition of the carcasses. Immanuel Velikovsky is a science writer who may be the greatest living advocate of a cosmic-disaster theory of history, somewhat like that of Cuvier mentioned above. In Velikovsky's view, most of the amazing and semimythical happenings described in ancient legends are not legends at all, but factual history. Thus such events as the dividing of the Red Sea for the ancient Hebrews and the story of the Great Flood that appears in folklore around the world can be accounted for by supposing that at various times the planet Earth has narrowly missed being knocked to fragments by other heavenly bodies such as a comet that later became the planet Venus or, at another period, the planet Mars. It is one of these near collisions that Velikovsky believes brought about the death of the mammoths, as well as other earth-shaking events. In his view, the mammoths were either suffocated or electrocuted by the violent gas storms that accompanied the disaster and were later quick-frozen when the formerly temperate lands of Siberia were suddenly converted to regions of polar cold.

Velikovsky's idea is certainly the most exciting and dramatic explanation of the frozen mammoths since the Hannibal's-elephants theory. If it were true, we would all have to rearrange our ideas about world history and the nature of the universe. Unfortunately for those of us who like colorful ideas, nearly all scientists are agreed that Velikovsky is mistaken. The reasons why Velikovsky's theories have not been accepted are complicated, but even if we limit ourselves to thinking about the mammoths, there is one big objection to the idea that they were the victims of a worldwide disaster. Why, if that were so, weren't all the other animals of Siberia frozen also? We know that the region was inhabited by many other kinds of animals, such as bears and reindeer, yet, except for one woolly rhinoceros, the only mummified creatures found in Siberia have been mammoths.* Since mammoths, being bigger than other animals, should be more difficult to freeze, not easier, it is hard to accept Velikovsky's theory—even if one believes it possible that Earth did once have a near collision with a comet or planet.

It may be that we are simply not able to account for the disappearance of the mammoths at the present time. The only other popular suggestion has been that the mammoths died

---

*Alaska, on the other hand, has yielded the frozen bodies of many species of animals, both modern and extinct.

out because of something called "racial old age." This means, simply, that species may reach a point in their development where they lose their vigor or their ability to adapt to changing conditions and so become extinct without any apparent outside cause. This would all be very well if we were able to say when and why one species falls victim to racial old age while others, such as the cockroach, live on for millions of years. The racial old age explanation amounts to saying the mammoths died because they died—leaving us right back where we started.

On the other hand, our main interest in the mammoths stems from the fact that they became mummies, not that they became extinct. We may not be able to account for the death of the species, but in some cases there is enough evidence to show quite clearly what happened to individual animals.

For example, the Hertz expedition's observations of the place where the Beresovska mammoth was found show that that particular river bank was a very dangerous place for a mammoth to be on that day more than twenty-five thousand years ago. As we know from the plants found in the animal's stomach, it was summer. Siberian summers are certainly not hot, but they are quite warm enough for certain hardy plants to grow and flower. They are also warm enough, in many cases, to melt snow. During the Ice Age, when the mammoths lived, Siberia and other northern areas went through several periods of alternately increasing and decreasing cold. When the cold came on the great Arctic ice sheets spread farther and farther south. Moving only a fraction of an inch each year, they advanced slowly until they covered large parts of Europe, Asia, and North America. Then a slightly warmer period would arrive, and the glaciers would as slowly inch back to the north. The summer day when our mammoth was taking his last meal apparently occurred during such a warm period. The mammoth, of course, knew nothing of this. He wandered onto an

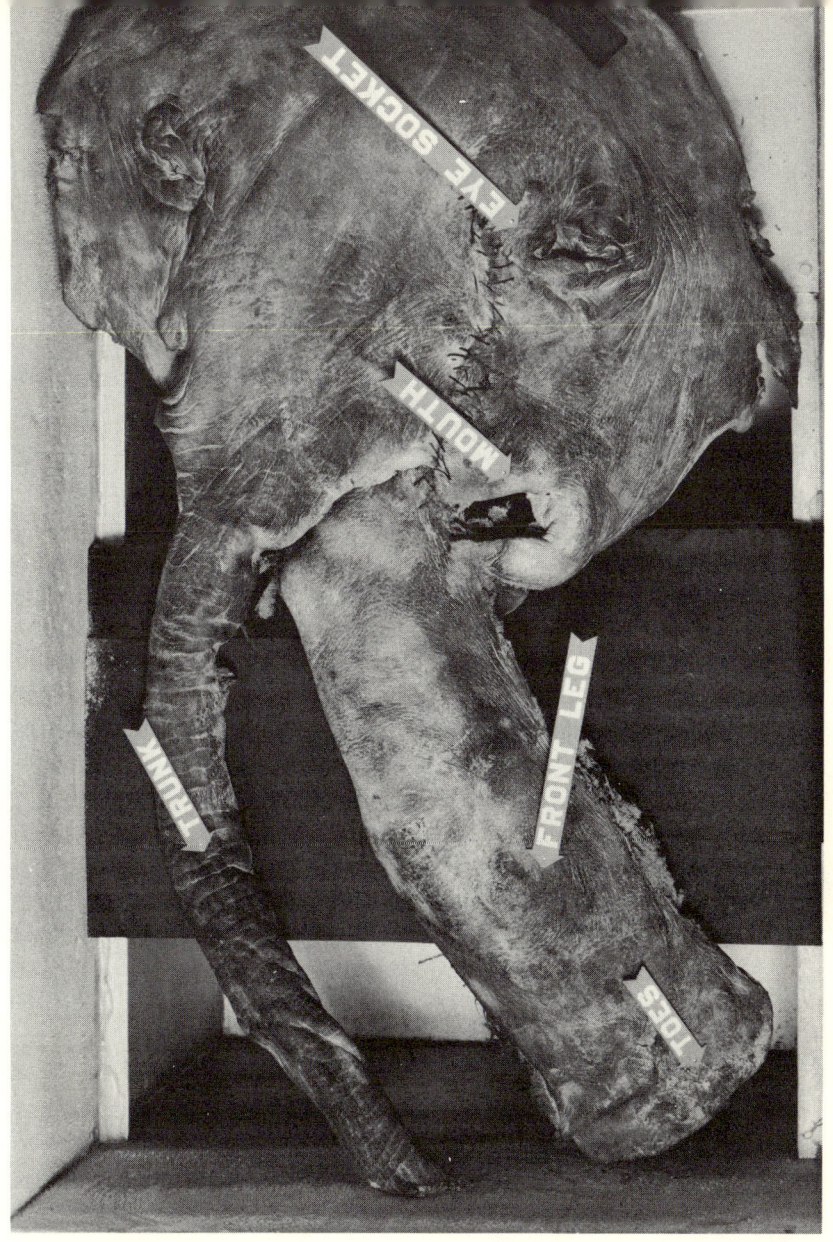

Well-preserved baby woolly mammoth, dug out of frozen earth in Cripple Creek, Alaska

area that looked, no doubt, just like the rest of the tundra. In fact, however, that piece of shrub-covered land was resting on top of a glacier. Over the thousands of years of the last ice invasion, soil had blown onto the glacier, plants had seeded and helped to form more soil until the place looked just like the firm ground around it. However, the glacier beneath it was no longer solid. The great mass of ice had cracked, softened, and been worn away until, under its thin covering of soil, it was crisscrossed with deep crevasses almost like trenches in the ice. The unwary mammoth weighed several tons and when he stepped onto one of these thin-soil layers that covered a crevasse, he fell straight through it. The place was, in fact, a perfect natural elephant trap. The geological condition of the earth and rocks in the area and the bones of the mammoth tell the story as clearly as if it had been written down at the time. The force of the fall must have broken the animal's ribs, his pelvis, and one front foot. Try as he would, he could not lever himself out of the deep gully. He died, either from injuries or from exhaustion, and the frozen ground around him preserved him just as he had fallen. A time machine could hardly give a more vivid picture of the event.

This scene, with variations, might have been repeated many times in the parts of Siberia where the geological conditions were right. If so, it would explain why only the heaviest animals in the region, the mammoth and the woolly rhinoceros, have turned up as frozen witnesses to the vanished Ice Age. It was to be many thousands of years before human beings would succeed in preserving their dead as perfectly as a series of Siberian accidents preserved the mammoths.

III
All the Best Egyptians

As far as we know, the people of ancient Egypt were the first to make artificial mummies. For more than four thousand years every Egyptian dreamed of having his body preserved after death and it has been estimated that about 700 *million* bodies actually were mummified in one way or another.

However, fortunately for the archaeologists (the men who dig up the remains of ancient civilizations), that does not mean that all those 700 million bodies were successfully preserved until modern times. The truth is that the Egyptians needed many centuries, even thousands of years, to learn the best methods of mummification. For in spite of the fact that the mammoths had already been lying for tens of thousands of years in their icy tombs, the Egyptians soon discovered that mummification was a very difficult art, requiring special skills and knowledge.

In fact, the Egyptians might never have gone in for mummification at all if they hadn't happened to live where they did. Just as the cold Arctic climate was responsible for preserving the mammoths, so the hot, dry sand of the North African desert probably made the first human mummies. The bodies of the earliest Egyptians were buried in much the same way the dead are buried the world over. However, instead of being in damp soil they were in desert sand and instead of decaying, the bodies simply dried out. It was a completely different process from that which led to the preservation of the mammoths, but it was nearly as effective.

We will probably never know exactly *how* it was that the Egyptians began to make mummies. However, one reasonable suggestion is that they got the idea in earliest times from seeing those sand-dried bodies. In any case, the record of the tombs shows us that it was a very long time before they learned to make mummies as good as the ones that were made by accident in the hot sand. They tried all kinds of ways of preserving the body, and some of them had exactly the opposite effect from what was intended.

The first stage in the development of mummification took place at the period of Egyptian history known as the second dynasty (about 3000 B.C.).* At this time the bodies were placed in wooden coffins shaped like houses, showing that the people already had the idea that the life after death was much like this life—the body would need a house to live in. Bodies usually lay on their left sides with the knees bent and were wrapped in bands of linen. The linen was meant to serve two purposes. It helped the body keep its shape and it was supposed to prevent decay. Unfortunately, the wrappings also kept the body away from the air and probably made it decay faster. The reason is that the bacteria that cause decay work best where it is damp and the bandages just helped keep the body from drying out. Most mummies of this period are in pretty bad condition. We might not even call them mummies if later events did not show us what the people who made them were trying to do.

---

*A dynasty is a family of rulers. There were thirty dynasties in Egypt before the year 332 B.C., when the country was conquered by Alexander the Great.

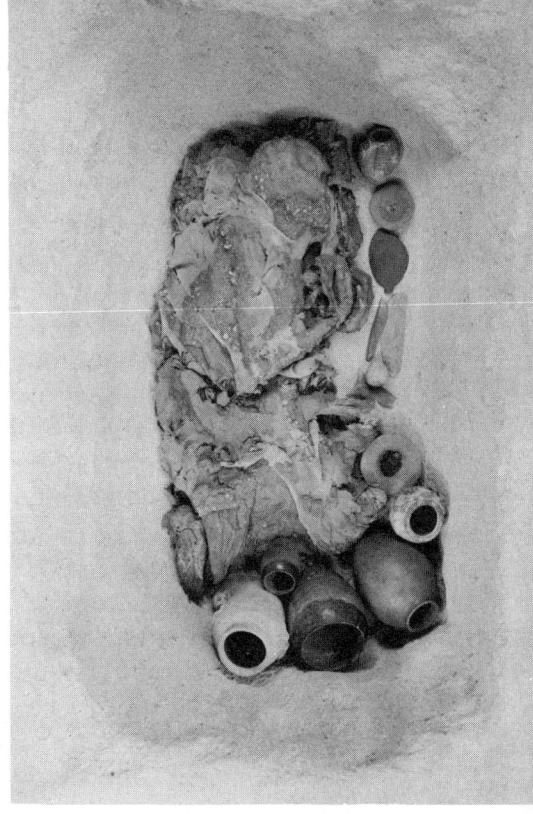

Very early tomb from Gebelein containing a natural mummy

In the period of Dynasties III through VI, about 2700–2400 B.C., a new idea was introduced. Perhaps the Egyptians had observed from the animals they killed for food that the first part of the body to decay is usually the internal organs—that is, the intestines, liver, kidneys, stomach, and so on. These organs are known as the viscera or "soft parts" of the body. Mummies of this period usually lie stretched out on their backs and have had the viscera removed, obviously with the purpose of slowing down the process of decay. But again, a reasonable idea didn't work very well. The viscera may be the *first* part of the body to decay, but all the rest, the muscles and skin and so on, will decay eventually unless something specific is done to stop them. Yet there was one improvement in the method of mummification during this period which may not have been much help in preserving the flesh but at least made the mummy look more lifelike. The linen bandages were now soaked in a resinous material resembling pine gum. When stiffened by resins the linen could be molded to show the shape of the body more clearly, particularly the face, and as time went on the mask that was formed of the stiffened linen was made more and more lifelike by painting the features of the dead person on it.

During the next several centuries, or until about 2000 B.C., Dynasties VII through XII, yet a different method was tried. Instead of removing the viscera through a slit in the lower body, a variety of substances was used *inside* the body. Not everyone agrees on just what these substances were or how they were used, however. That is because during the four thousand years or so since the mummies of that period were made the materials that were used in the mummification have become so fused with the materials of the body tissues themselves that sometimes not even a chemist can tell which is which or what they were in the beginning.

Fortunately, we have other ways of finding out exactly what substances were used for mummification at this period. For one thing, the Egyptians left behind them, in tombs and other places, a very large number of books and documents written on papyrus, the earliest form of paper. Some of these records concern the art of mummification, although they are often unclear. Another source is the writings of later historians such as the Greek Herodotus. We say "later" because Herodotus lived long after 2000 B.C. Nevertheless, he died about 425 B.C., at a time when mummification was still being done, and he had been able to talk to living Egyptians who were supposed to know the method.

Herodotus tells us some very interesting things about *who* was mummified, as well as about *how*. For although every

Egyptian believed in the Kingdom of the Dead and wished to be prepared for the life after death, by no means everyone could afford to be mummified. Throughout Egyptian history, the majority of the people—slaves and common folk—were given simple grave burial in the vast cemeteries or necropolises of the time. Only the richer few could afford preservation of the body, and Herodotus describes three different methods of mummification, one for minor court officials, one for nobles, and one (the most expensive, of course) for the greatest nobles and royalty.

The honor of mummification was not reserved solely for human beings, however. An extraordinary variety of mammals, birds, reptiles, and even insects was also preserved. One might think that the idea behind the practice was that human beings wanted animal companions in the afterlife, but that does not seem to have been the case. Cat lovers will often claim that the Egyptians loved cats so much that they went

Mummified cats

MUMMIES

into mourning when their pets died, entered burning buildings to save them, and so on. The truth is more complicated. The Egyptians did not keep cats, or hounds or crocodiles or vultures or any of the other creatures that were mummified, solely as pets, though they may well have become very found of their cats. The main reason why certain animals were given so much care was that they were connected with various gods. Most of the major Egyptian gods are pictured as having animal heads. For example, the goddess Bast has the head of a cat, the god Horus that of a falcon, and the god Anubis that of a jackal. Thus the cat was sacred to Bast, the falcon to Horus, and the jackal to Anubis. Certain cities worshipped one or another of the gods in particular, and kept the appropriate sacred animals in their temples. When they died, the sacred creatures were given royal burial.

Among the creatures mummified in this way were monkeys, dogs, lions, wolves, foxes, hyenas, bears, shrewmice, ichneumons (a kind of weasel), deer, goats, sheep, cattle, hippopotamuses, vultures, eagles, hawks, owls, ibises, geese, swallows, crocodiles, toads, monitor lizards, adders, asps and other snakes, carp, pike, perch and other fish, bats, scarab beetles and other insects, eggs of various kinds, and even plants such as the lotus, onion, and sycamore.

As to the exact methods used in making mummies, we know from the Egyptian papyruses and the writings of Herodotus that one of the things used was a mineral salt called natron. In those days natron was easily found in several regions of Egypt. It was a coarse, whitish stuff that looked a little like lumps of table salt, which was actually one of the things in it.*
The natron was probably intended to help preserve the body

---

*Table salt is known chemically as sodium chloride. Natron is a mixture of sodium carbonate and sodium bicarbonate, with small amounts of sodium chloride and sodium sulfate.

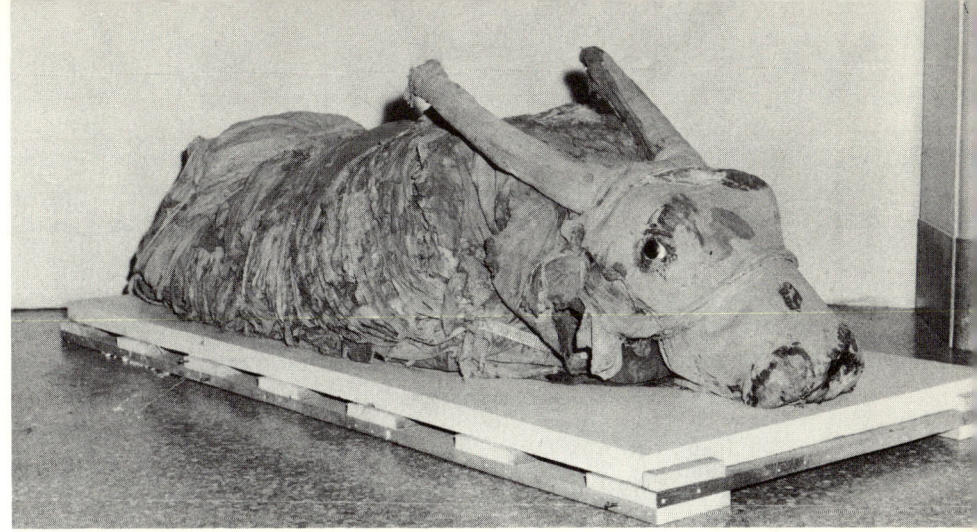
Mummy of a bull

just as table salt is used in preserving meat and fish. If so, the Egyptians of this period were on the right track, although the mummies they produced were far from perfect. The other important material for mummification was more mysterious. Herodotus called it "oil of cedar" and since there is an oil of this name that can be made from cedar wood, there should be no problem. The trouble is that most doctors and chemists agree that the substance we call cedar oil is too weak to be very useful in mummification. It is much more probable that Herodotus really meant something like turpentine. Today we are most familiar with turpentine as a material used to dissolve oily materials like paint. However, turpentine might possibly be useful in mummification because it also helps to dry things out and might act as a disinfectant to slow down the growth of decay-producing bacteria. In any case, natron and "oil of cedar" apparently continued to play an important part in Egyptian mummification. Mineral pitch, or bitumen, was also often used.

A mummy and mummy case

Still, the mummies made by these methods weren't nearly as good as they might have been. We sometimes find recognizable faces, but the rest of the body was often reduced to a blackened mass that can hardly be separated from its wrappings. Improvements were needed.

During the twelfth dynasty various old and new methods were tried, without much success. For a while the viscera were again removed through a slit in the lower body, but this worked no better than before.

It was not until the seventeenth dynasty and later (about 1500 B.C.) that we find the first examples of the method that was to bring the art of mummification to its highest point. Here again the internal organs, including the lungs and brain, were

Canopic jars

removed from the body.* The body cavities were sometimes treated with cedar oil, bitumen, or other supposed preservatives. More often they were filled with a packing of linen and resin, the same material that had been used in the outer wrapping of the mummy for centuries. This had the tremendous advantage of insuring that the body would not entirely collapse and shrivel like a glove without a hand inside.

From this point on the art of mummification improved rapidly. It had taken the Egyptians well over fifteen hundred years to produce mummies that were nearly as lasting as the original, accidental ones produced by the hot, dry sand. Now they went on to refine their methods, using a wide variety of other packing materials, such as lichen, sawdust, or a mixture

---

*As before, they were carefully preserved and buried in the same tombs. Usually each organ was placed in a separate jar, whose cover was carved with the head of the particular god who was believed to influence that part of the body. These jars are called canopic jars and, like all other objects found in the tombs, they are sometimes quite beautiful.

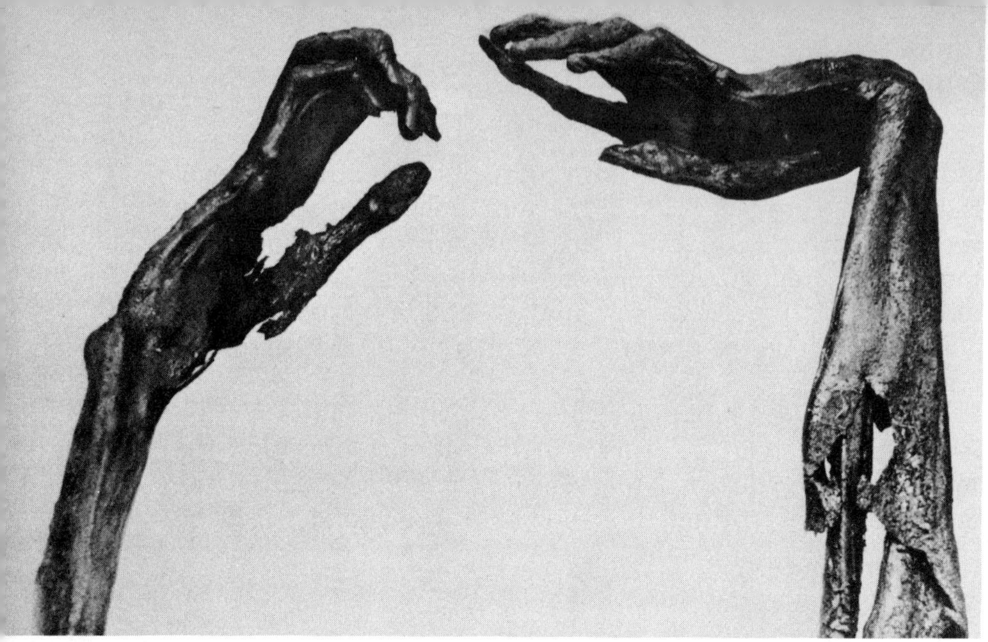

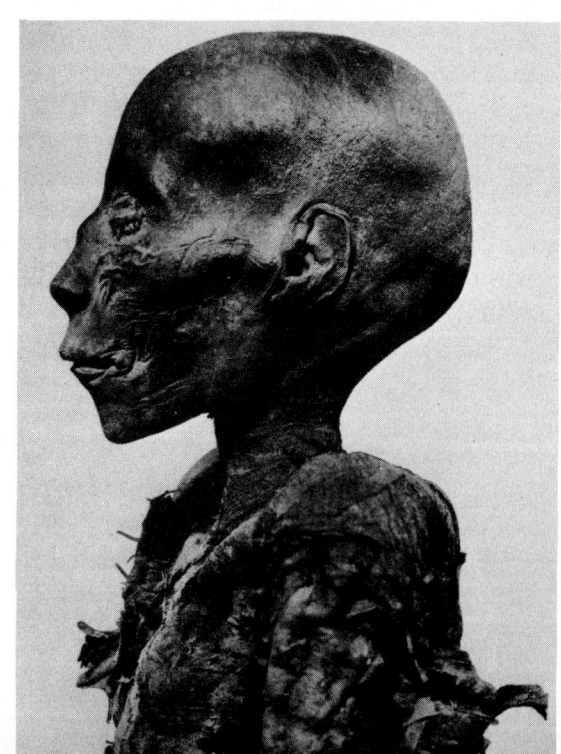

Hands of mummy,
Dynasty XVII

Thoutmosis I—
mummy of the
XVIII Dynasty

of natron and animal fat. Some sources say that mummies of this period were first dried in the sun, though various modern researchers have suggested that exposure to the sun would merely have encouraged normal decay. Whatever the case, mummies of the nineteenth and twentieth dynasties are in general much better preserved and more natural than earlier ones.

The very best mummies are probably those of the twenty-first dynasty (about 1059 B.C.). It was at that time that the mummy-makers learned to pack mud under the skin of the face and hands, so that the dried skin was almost stretched

Queen Notmit, Dynasty XXI

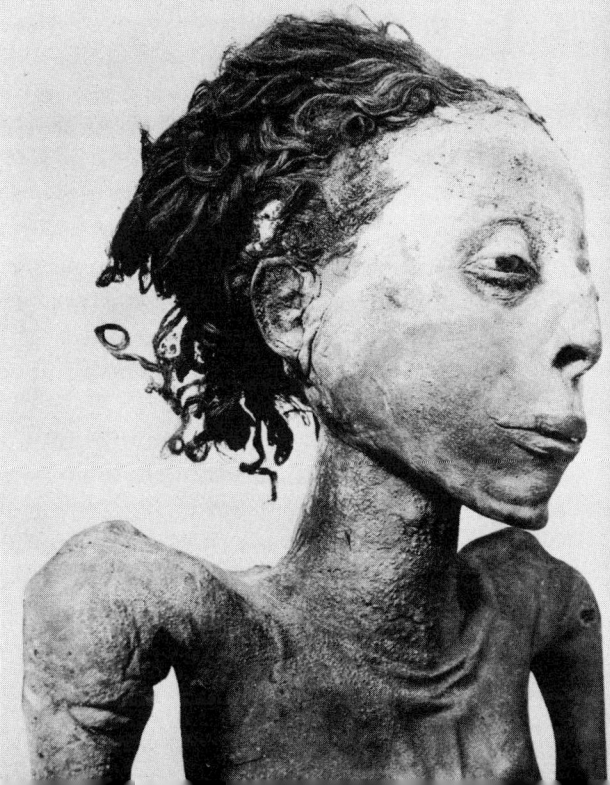

Nsitanebashrou, Dynasty XXI–XXII

over a clay sculpture of the living person. This was really the last word in keeping the shape of the body. Mummies of this period are almost as lifelike as a good statue showing the person asleep. Those who could afford to be preserved this way, for the process was very expensive, must have been greatly comforted by the assurance that their spirits would last as long in the next world as their bodies in this one.

The final period in the history of Egyptian mummification was one of slow decline. It had always been the custom, as we shall see, to enclose the mummy in a series of body-shaped coffins decorated with masks of the dead person, magical formulas written in hieroglyphics, and even, in the case of rulers and nobles, fabulous quantities of gold and jewels. However, during the later centuries the wrapping of the mummy seems to have become more important than the preservation of the body. Often the body was simply encased in pitch, while care and attention were lavished on the portrait mask that covered the face. Today we may be rather glad that this was so, since masks of those centuries (when Egyptian artists were under the influence of Greek painters) are among the most natural and realistic portraits we have from ancient times.

The end of mummification in Egypt did not come for many centuries, although the custom had been opposed by some of the early Christian groups in the country. It was not until Egypt was largely converted to the religion of Islam, in the seventh century A.D., that the making of mummies was finally given up completely. It had been almost the sole method of disposing of the dead in the country for over forty-five hundred years.

The fact that mummification lasted so long in Egypt is only one of the things that show how important the idea was to the people of the period. Everything about the way the dead were treated suggests that death was almost more important than life in the minds of the ancient Egyptians. It was not just the

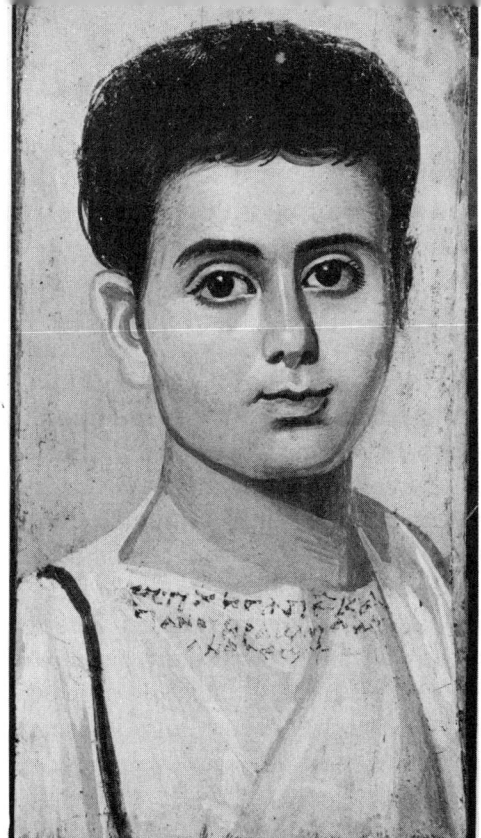

Portrait panel from a mummy of the second century A.D.

appearance of the living that had to be imitated or preserved in the next world. Nearly every aspect of the dead person's lifetime surroundings was provided for or duplicated in the tomb and funeral arrangements. Egyptian cemeteries were often known as cities of the dead, and that was not a bad name for them. Except in the case of the very poorest persons, each body, whether mummified or not, was buried with an assortment of objects for use in the next world. If the dead person had been a humble worker these might be merely some dishes of food (sometimes actual grain, sometimes clay models of foodstuffs), a favorite weapon or household implement, some pieces of clothing or ornaments. But when the body was that of a member of the royal family, the furnishings of the tomb were magnificent and luxurious beyond belief. The pharaohs of Egypt were provided with clothing by the chestful, jars of precious oils, caskets of jewels, gold and gem-studded weapons of war, private altars for the worship of the gods, musical instruments and gaming pieces for entertainment, and large supplies of food. Furthermore, it is plain that they did not imagine they would be alone in the land of the dead. Many clay and wooden models of servants and slaves are also found in the tombs—boatmen, torchbearers, scribes, serving maids, chariot drivers. The ruler was to be served as royally in death as he had been in life. Even the less important person was nearly always provided with one such figure, made of clay, glazed pottery, stone, or occasionally wood. This was the *ushabti* and it was believed to perform an even more useful job than all the royal servants combined. It was the ushabti's role to answer for its

Model boat from a tomb of the XI Dynasty

owner whenever he was called upon by the gods to do some work in the afterlife. By magic, the ushabti figure was supposed to bear the fatigue of those labors, thus saving the true body for a life of ease.

The ushabti was by no means the only magical device of importance in the Egyptian view of death. Not only was the whole idea of mummification a kind of magic way of cheating death, but the tomb and even the wrappings on the mummy itself were carefully and elaborately protected by charms and religious objects. The most common of these was the scarab, a small stone or gem carved in the likeness of the scarab beetle. This insect was viewed as a symbol of rebirth because it has the unusual habit of laying its eggs inside balls of animal dung. The emergence of a live beetle from the apparently dead matter led to the belief that the scarab could give man a similar power to return from the dead. There were actually dozens of other kinds of sacred objects that were often buried with mummies in order to assure their future welfare. There were also a great many magical formulas that were either written on the inner and outer mummy cases themselves or inscribed in papyrus scrolls and left in the tomb so that the dead could read them. The most famous collection of these formulas forms a kind of instruction book which tells the dead person how to act in the Kingdom of the Dead and is known as The Book of the Dead.

It is plain that the things that were put into the Egyptian tombs, both the magical items and the useful ones, were valuable and often beautiful in their own right, apart from the importance they had for the future life of their owners. And since human beings are the way they are, it is not surprising that robbing tombs has been almost as popular a pastime as making mummies in Egypt, from the earliest times right up to the present.

Oddly enough, the final effect of such tomb-robbing was not all bad. First of all, it seems likely that the Egyptians would

Ushabti of Seti I   *King Seti I, Dynasty XIX*

not have become so good at mummification if they had had no way of knowing how well their attempts were succeeding. Naturally, no pious or respectable person would rob a tomb.

But the fact that tombs certainly *were* robbed on occasion suggests that the mummy-makers *could* have gotten information about the state of earlier mummies found in the tombs. If they had had to rely on accidental uncovering of graves to give them their knowledge, they might never have known which techniques were promising and which did not work at all.

If tomb-robbing had an effect upon the techniques of mummification, it had an equally important effect on the history of medicine. The Egyptians were known as the best physicians of their time and some peoples of other lands believed the reason was that the Egyptians used a superior kind of magic. A much more likely explanation is that Egyptian doctors and embalmers had the opportunity to study the human

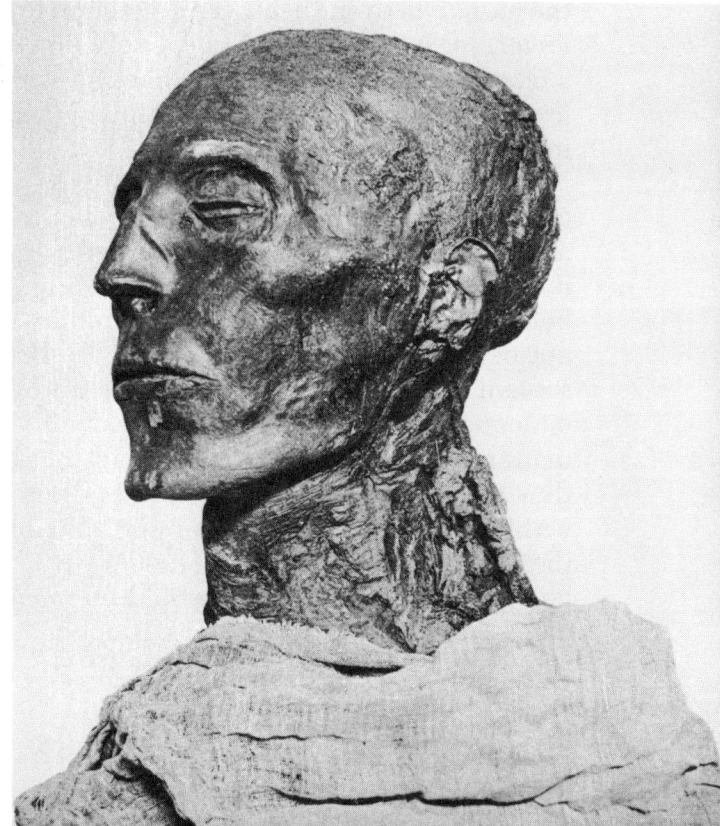

Head of Seti I

body in a way that few, if any, other ancient nations permitted. That is, they were able to study the internal organs at the time when they were removed during mummification.

In many other cultures it was absolutely forbidden to cut into a dead body. The fear of doing such a thing is not hard to explain. First, we know that people are afraid of being cut when they are alive, mainly because it hurts. This leads to the idea that the dead or the "souls" of the dead might be hurt by being cut, even though there is no evidence at all to show that that is so. Next comes the thought that if we hurt the dead in this way, they might come back and hurt us. In other words, those who hold this belief are really afraid that the dead person's "ghost" might come back and take revenge. Finally, laws against cutting into bodies were sometimes passed for the purpose of preventing witches or magicians from using parts of the human body in their magic. One can imagine that a human finger, for example, would be a very powerful thing to use in a magic potion. (The three witches in Shakespeare's *Macbeth* used "nose of Turk and Tartar's lips" along with their "eye of newt and toe of frog.")

It is interesting that the Egyptians, who were so deeply concerned with preserving the body's outward appearance for all eternity, do not seem to have been at all unwilling to cut it up and even to remove organs if it would help them to make better, more lifelike and lasting mummies. They obviously did not believe that what was done to the body in order to preserve it could be called "hurting" it, and they must also have understood that the dead body was quite without feeling, no matter what the soul might or might not be like. Thus it was they who first observed that certain diseases were connected with certain organs such as the stomach or liver and that when the dead person had complained of certain symptoms before he died, a particular organ would be found to be diseased or damaged when the body was cut open.

In later centuries, Greek travelers like Herodotus brought back to Greece with them the idea that physicians should study the inside of the body as well as the outside. The ancient Greek physicians then went on to carry the knowledge of the Egyptians even further, and the writings of such great doctors as Hippocrates (about 460–370 B.C.) became the foundation of all medical practice in western Europe for the next fifteen hundred years and more. It is strange to think that the tremendous effort the Egyptians spent on mummification may have been of more benefit to the living, through the medical knowledge it produced, than to the dead.

IV
The Young King's Treasure

At the end of the last chapter, we mentioned two effects of the early practice of tomb-robbing. There was a further change that the thieves helped bring about, one that played a major role in preserving many mummies into the twentieth century.

The more valuable a thing is, the harder someone will try to steal it. And the harder the thief tries, the harder its owner will work to prevent him. Thus as Egypt grew into the richest and most powerful kingdom of its day, the contents of its tombs became more and more dazzling and the measures taken to prevent robbery grew more and more complex. The very earliest tombs had been simple holes in the earth or the sand, followed by the placing of the bodies in house-shaped wooden chests. After that tombs called *mastabas* were carved out of rock or dug in gravel. But by a fairly early date, around the time of the third and fourth dynasties (2800 to 2600 B.C.), the builders had begun to protect the royal tombs with pyramids, aboveground brick structures that both marked the place of the tomb and made it much more difficult to get into. The inside structure of the pyramids makes it plain that their builders were perfectly aware that robbers would try their best to steal the treasures within. They constructed dead-end passageways, hidden doors, and false treasure chambers designed to mislead the thieves. The trouble with this approach to tomb-building was that, although it provided a magnificent monument to the power of the dead pharaoh, it also provided the clearest kind of signpost to the location of a fabulous treasure. No amount of false entrances, it turned out, served to prevent the robbers from finding their way into the heart of the tomb. And when they got there they often actually destroyed the mummy in their haste to remove its magical gold and jewelled amulets.

The horror that this practice roused in the mighty lords of Egypt may well be imagined. The whole vast pyramid, with its chapels and antechambers, passages and storage rooms, existed solely for the eternal welfare and protection of the mummy, without which the spirit would wander naked in the afterlife. If the mummy was to be damaged by wicked men with no respect for religion, then other ways of hiding and protecting it would have to be found.

It was probably for reasons of safety, therefore, that the building of pyramids was given up rather early in Egyptian history, around 1500 B.C. Instead, the rulers of Egypt began making their tombs in chambers hollowed out of the rocky cliffs in a place that came to be known as the Valley of the Kings. Nearby were the Valley of the Queens and the Valley of the Nobles. These rock tombs, though no less magnificently furnished than the pyramids, were harder to find. The reason, of course, was that the only outward sign of the tomb's location was a single entrance in the natural rock wall or in the valley floor, and the builders did everything they possibly could to conceal and wall up that entrance. Another means of keeping the tomb secret was more drastic. Since it took a great amount of labor to build a royal tomb, it was obvious that the workmen

Typical excavation of a tomb in the Valley of the Kings

employed to do the job could, if they wished, reveal the tomb's location. In at least some cases there is evidence that the construction workers were murdered after the job was completed. "Three can keep a secret, if two of them are dead," says the proverb. In such a case, the pharaoh for whom the tomb was built was obviously dead before it was used, and if the slaves who knew the secret were also put out of the way, that left only the architect himself to know the true route to the gold-encrusted coffin. Perhaps it was assumed that the architects themselves would not tell, if only because their reputations rested on their skill in designing theft-proof tombs.

In spite of all precautions, tomb-robbery continued to be

THE YOUNG KING'S TREASURE

something of a local industry in those parts of Egypt. Four thousand years of betrayal, persistent searching, and lucky accident led to such a high rate of success that modern archaeologists have found that it is a rare tomb indeed that has not been robbed of at least some of its riches. Still, it might be said that by their efforts the thieves encouraged the priests and rulers to take extraordinary care in concealment, so that a few mummies have been found undamaged—saved for us to study rather than to steal.

There is no better way to get an idea of how a royal tomb was prepared to receive its mummy than by examining a particular example. The tomb of the boy King Tut-ankh-Amen contained neither the best preserved mummy nor (probably) the richest furnishings in history. However, the story of its discovery in 1922 is so dramatic and caused so much worldwide excitement that it is almost impossible to think of mummies without thinking of Tut-ankh-Amen or "King Tut" as he was popularly called thirty-three hundred years after his death.

The famous tomb was built in the eighteenth dynasty in the Valley of the Kings (about 1350 B.C.). In the space below the steep cliffs the remains of tombs and tomb construction lie so thick on the ground that it is almost impossible to tell where one site begins and another leaves off. Stone slabs, sets of steps, broken pottery, unexplained holes in the earth, and rock walls make an incredible jumble, a jumble that was even more confusing in 1917 when Howard Carter and Lord Carnarvon first began to dig there seriously.

Carter and Carnarvon were not the first students of ancient Egypt to dig in the valley. European archaeologists had been interested in the place for at least a century and some very important tombs had been uncovered. However, the two Englishmen were the first to work on the site in a systematic manner, going over the ground foot by foot, and even inch by inch. They made an excellent team for this sort of work. Lord Carnarvon was an educated and enthusiastic nobleman with a private fortune, while Carter was a methodical and experienced professional archaeologist. They were interested not only in spectacular and valuable tomb finds but in anything and everything that would add to the world's knowledge of ancient Egypt.

Nevertheless, it happened that Carter and Carnarvon, rather than any of the researchers who had gone before them, were the ones to stumble on a stone step leading downward into the rock beneath some ancient workmen's huts. That important event was not entirely a matter of luck. The expedition had already been digging in the valley for several seasons without uncovering anything of special interest. Lord Carnarvon was not even present at the finding of the step, on November 4, 1922. He had returned to London a few weeks before. Carter, however, knew immediately that this one stone might lead to a major find. He hastily sent for Carnarvon to return to the site and went on with the digging. A few more days of work brought them to the bottom of a flight of fifteen steps which ended in a sealed stone door.

At that point, Carter later recalled, he wasn't certain he should go on with the work. For although the steps undoubtedly led to a tomb entrance, it was plain from the condition of the stones and the seals on the door that the archaeologists were not the first to come that way. At some period, not later than the reign of Ramses IV, when the overhead workmen's huts had been built, intruders had entered the tomb not once but twice. Should the digging go on? It might be that the end of all their work would be an empty coffin and a rifled treasure chamber.

Yet Carter did decide to go on. The passageway behind the door had been found to be filled with rubble from floor to ceiling. The archaeologist reasoned that the robbers would not

THE YOUNG KING'S TREASURE

have gone to so much trouble if there were nothing left to protect. Lord Carnarvon returned to the site, accompanied by his daughter, and everyone waited anxiously for developments.

The job of clearing the thirty-two feet of rubble-filled passage that lay behind the door was a long one. It was November 26 before the workmen came upon a second door. Like the first, it showed signs of having been used by robbers. But now, with any luck, the excavators would learn whether the tomb was only an empty shell. With the greatest care, Carter made a small opening in one corner. He pushed through a testing rod and found emptiness on the other side. Not another rubble-filled passage, then. Next the air issuing from the tomb was tested with candle flames to ensure that no poisonous gases had developed during the thirty centuries and more since it was last opened. Then, as excited workmen and visitors crowded around, Carter held up a candle for his first look at the interior of the tomb of Tut-ankh-Amen. The silence that followed was breathless. Finally Lord Carnarvon could stand it no longer. "Can you see anything?" he asked urgently.

Turning away from the hole, Carter answered in one short sentence. "Yes," he said, "wonderful things."

It took another day to clear the sealed doorway, which was three and a half feet thick. It was only then that the party could realize what Carter had meant by "wonderful things." The room beyond the door was packed with objects, any one of which could have been the proudest display of a museum's Egyptian wing. A gilded throne, three gilded couches decorated with animal heads, alabaster vases, painted chests, two large royal statues, shrines, clothing, and carvings—the whole treasure was not only incredibly valuable but incredibly beautiful as well. Each object was in the finest artistic style of its time, painted, carved, embossed, or inlaid with scenes and designs of the greatest grace and loveliness.

MUMMIES

So absorbed were the discoverers in the scene that they did not immediately notice two remarkable facts. First, though robbers had plainly been here, as could be seen from a scattering of objects on the floor, the room was so full that *hardly anything of importance could have been taken.* What could the thieves have been looking for that would seem to them more desirable than the riches that lay all around them?

Second, the one most obvious and important object, the one thing they had expected to find, was not to be seen. Where was the actual mummy of Tut-ankh-Amen, with its surround-

Detail from the royal chair showing Tut-ankh-Amen and his wife in a garden

ing coffins and sarcophagus? This must not be the main chamber of the tomb at all, but only a sort of antechamber. There must be more to be uncovered. A careful search revealed that there were indeed *two* more sealed doors, one in the middle of the wall to the right of the entrance, between the two statues, and a smaller one near the far left-hand corner.

Less careful and dedicated archaeologists than Carter and Carnarvon might have been tempted to push on into the rest of the tomb at this point. In fact, it seems hard to believe that they had the self-control not to do so. But there were very good reasons why, instead of going immediately to the heart of the treasure, the leaders decided not only to leave the antechamber but to fill up the passageway and secure the outer doorway with a heavy steel door before proceeding with the excavation. So for thirteen days the tomb stood silent, carefully guarded against anyone who might have it in mind to bring the tradition of tomb-robbing up to date.

Carter and Carnarvon had realized that the objects found were of such artistic and historical value, and in many cases so fragile, that to charge on without preparation would result in the loss of much vital information and perhaps even in damage to the treasures themselves. Fabrics and wooden objects, for example, would have to be carefully packed and treated with preservatives by experts before they could safely be moved from the site. The same was true of the delicate gold leaf and faience (glazed pottery) objects. And finally, it would be necessary to have expert help before the excavators could even move some of the larger and more breakable pieces.

As soon as the world learned of the find, other Egyptologists and specialists immediately sent offers of help. The Metropolitan Museum of Art in New York gave the services of a photographer and two artists. The director of the Egyptian government's chemical department came in person to lend a hand, as did an inscriptions expert from the University of Chicago.

Now the painstaking clearing of the antechamber began. Every object had to be examined, described, numbered, marked as to location, preserved, and packed before it could leave the scene. The antechamber was cleaned out by the middle of February, 1923, and only then did Carter and Carnarvon turn to the unsealing of the large door between the two statues. (A brief investigation of the smaller door had shown that it led to a little annex to the main room, filled with objects much like those in the main room but badly scattered about by the robbers.)

On Friday, February 17, some twenty persons gathered in the antechamber to watch the disclosing of the tomb's final secret. Few were even willing to guess what might be behind the door. The objects already found were so fabulous that it hardly seemed possible that there was nothing of importance behind the door at all. Yet robbers might have looted the room of everything movable, explaining why they had not bothered with the treasure in the antechamber. Or perhaps the doorway led only to a blank wall, where another room had been planned but never constructed. It could be that the "antechamber" had been the burial chamber after all and that the missing mummy had been removed to safekeeping by pious priests sometime after the original burial. This had been known to happen in other cases, where the priests apparently hoped to save the mummy from damage by robbers.

Like an audience at a play, the visitors and the officials sat down in rows of chairs while Carter began the task of unsealing the door. "The temptation to stop and peer inside at every moment was irresistible," he wrote later. Yet he did resist it, picking away at the first layer of stones and taking the greatest care that none of them should fall into the next room and damage the objects, if any, that lay inside.

At last a reasonable-sized hole had been made, and once again, as it had been at the opening of the outer door all those

Funeral goods in the interior of the antechamber

months ago, the air was tense with excitement. Carter shone a flashlight through the hole and, also as before, found the way ahead solidly blocked. But not with stones and rubble. Whichever way he turned the light the same bright gleam came back at him. The doorway was nearly filled by a wall of solid gold.

Quickly but cautiously, Carter removed the rest of the stones. As the gold surface was slowly revealed it became clear to the archaeologists in the party that they had definitely found the burial chamber and that what they were looking at with such astonishment was an amazingly large, costly, and beautiful shrine of the kind often built over the sarcophagus.

Now there was another tension-filled delay. Not even a great gold shrine was going to make Carter forget the painstaking requirements of archaeology. On the threshold of the burial chamber lay the beads of a broken necklace, probably dropped by the tomb-robbers thousands of years ago. Each bead had to be gathered up before the chamber could be entered. Then another discovery was made. The level of the floor in the burial chamber was over three feet below that of the antechamber and the space between the shrine and the chamber wall was only about fifteen inches. It was an awkward position, but Carter, Carnarvon, and the chemist Dr. Lucas managed to enter and get the first look at the full extent of the shrine. Later measurement showed it to be seventeen feet long, eleven feet wide, and nine feet high, covered with gold or blue glazed panels showing protective magic symbols.

The great question was whether the archaeologists were really the first to get this far into the burial chamber. There was no way of telling from the doors of the shrine, as they were bolted but not sealed. Eagerly, Carter opened the doors and came upon another set. There was a second shrine inside the first. And the doors of this second shrine were both bolted and sealed.

The investigators knew then that the robbers had not been there before them. They were within reach of the only undisturbed royal sarcophagus discovered in the Valley of the Kings up to that time. The three men then turned to the other end of the room, where they had noticed another doorway. It proved to open into a small room that was filled with yet more treasure. Especially noticeable was a golden chest in the shape of a shrine surrounded by four goddesses. The figures seemed to be pleading with the intruders not to disturb the rest of the king who lay nearby. As the archaeologists left the chamber so that others might come in, they felt awe and a kind of reverence for the people who had lavished such care on their dead ruler.

It was now the winter of 1923–24, over a year since a single stone step had been found in the dry Egyptian earth.

Work was begun on the tremendous job of clearing enough space so that the sarcophagus that surely lay within the shrines could at last be opened. First the brick wall between the anteroom and the burial chamber had to be removed so that the shrines could be taken carefully apart and set up again elsewhere. The moment came when the doors of the second shrine were opened, to reveal a third shrine within. Experience would have led Carter to believe that the sarcophagus would be inside the third shrine. "With suppressed excitement I carefully cut the cord, removed the precious seal, drew back the blots, and opened the doors, when a fourth shrine was revealed, similar in design and even more brilliant in workmanship than the last.... An indescribable moment for an archaeologist! What was beneath and what did that fourth shrine contain? With intense excitement I drew back the blots of the last and unsealed doors; they slowly swung open, and there, filling the entire area within ... stood an immense yellow quartzite sarcophagus, intact, just as the pious hands had left it."

Next the four shrines had to be removed from the burial chamber, a job that took eighty-four days by itself.

But now, just as the workers were ready to open the sarcophagus, work on the tomb was again delayed. Following the unfortunate death of Lord Carnarvon, a dispute had arisen with the Egyptian government over the extension of the expedition's original permission to dig and over the division of the finds. The last is a common source of difficulty. Do archaeological treasures belong to the country where they are found, to the discoverers themselves (although Carter and Carnarvon were making no such claim), or to the institutions in other countries, such as museums and universities, that provide the money for the work? In this case an international commission had to be called to settle the dispute before the job of uncovering the mummy could at last begin.

A block and tackle had to be used to raise the huge stone lid of the sarcophagus. Inside was a so-called anthropoid coffin whose lid was molded into a portrait of King Tut-ankh-Amen. Gilded like the shrines that had enclosed it, it was inlaid with semiprecious aragonite, obsidian, and lapis lazuli glass. The hands were crossed on the chest and held the traditional symbols of royalty, the crook and the flail. The maker of this portrait had wanted to show Tut-ankh-Amen as a great and powerful ruler and he had succeeded. But those who gathered around the coffin also saw something else—a tiny wreath of flowers, faded but still showing some of their colors, that had apparently been placed on the coffin just before the sarcophagus was closed. Perhaps they had been the last gift of the pharaoh's young wife. They were certainly a touching reminder that the incredible magnificence of the tomb had not drowned out the genuine feelings of love and grief in the minds of the mourners.

Carter examining second coffin of Tut-ankh-Amen

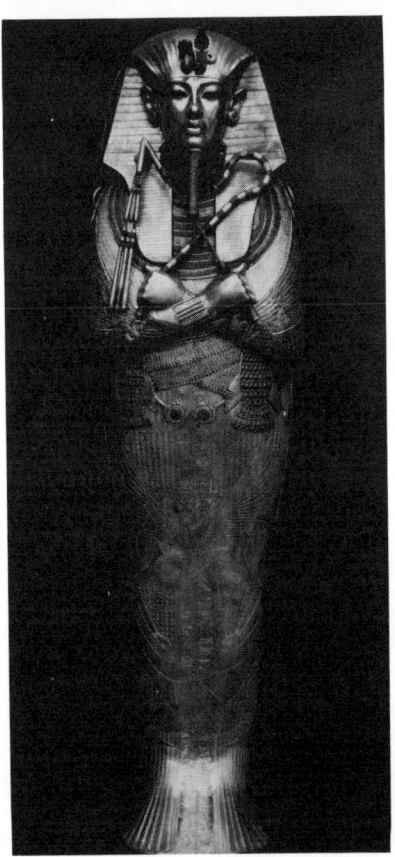

The innermost gold coffin of Tut-ankh-Amen

The work of opening the coffins went on. Closely nested inside the first coffin and covered with a linen shroud was a second one, also bearing a portrait of the pharaoh. This was just what the archaeologists would have expected, from their knowledge of other tombs, but several remarked on the unusual heaviness of the nested coffins. They were about to discover the reason.

When the third coffin was revealed, it was found to be made of solid gold, rather than of wood covered with thin gold sheets as the others had been. Over six feet long and about a fifth of an inch thick, it was probably one of the largest gold objects ever made.

MUMMIES

The men in the burial chamber were naturally excited by the discovery of the golden coffin, but their feelings were somewhat dampened when they noticed something odd. The entire space between the second and third coffins had apparently been filled with some sticky liquid that had hardened over the centuries into a solid mass. What would this mean for the condition of the mummy within? It seemed likely that the stuff had originally been some sort of sacred oil or unguent. Before going further, Dr. Lucas undertook a rough chemical analysis to find out what the material was and how it might best be handled. The main ingredients seemed to be some sort of fat, some sort of resin, and wood pitch. The stuff could be dissolved and cleaned off the outside of the coffin, but what it might have done to the mummy was impossible to guess.

Now on November 11, 1925, thirty-three hundred years after his death and eight years after Carter and Carnarvon had begun their investigation of the Valley of the Kings, the body of Tut-ankh-Amen was again exposed to view.

In an exploration that had been so full of amazing and unexpected discoveries, it was strange that the actual mummy should be something of a disappointment. The zeal that had led the funeral attendants nearly to soak the mummy in costly oils had not produced the desired result. Below the gleaming gold mask that covered the mummy's head and shoulders, the observers saw a blackened and almost shapeless mass. Only the head and feet were partially free of the stuff. It appeared that wherever the unguent had touched, the chemical changes brought about by time had produced heat and the result was almost the same as if the body had been burned. Wryly, Carter and his companions realized that those mummies that had been disturbed by robbers and by priests trying to save them from robbers had often fared better than this one, which had remained untouched. In the process of removal, *they* had been saved from the action of the unguents.

THE YOUNG KING'S TREASURE

Nevertheless, it was important to examine what remained of the mummy as thoroughly as possible. Tut-ankh-Amen's exact age and the cause of his death were unknown and the body might offer clues to the answers to these and other historical questions. With infinite care the mummy was unwound, although in some places the unguent had become so hard that it had to be chiseled away. No fewer than 143 magical amulets and pieces of jewelry were found inside the wrappings, each one having been placed there to do its part in protecting the body from damage and decay. When the wrappings were all off, it was found that the damage from the unguent was even worse than had been expected. Not only the bandages, but even the flesh and bones had been turned to carbon as if burned. Of all the parts of the body, only the head was in reasonably good condition. When the last pieces of linen were removed the onlookers at last saw the face of the young man whose name had been at the center of all their thoughts for years of painstaking work. Tut-ankh-Amen had not been a great king by any standard. He had had a confused reign whose short span made it impossible to know whether he might have made his mark on the world if he had lived longer. But now, looking at Tut-ankh-Amen's face, it was possible to believe some of the tributes that had been written to him in his lifetime. The gentle and sensitive impression conveyed by the portrait masks was repeated in their original. Carter wrote that the face was "refined and cultured, the features well-formed, especially the clearly marked lips." From later examination of the skeleton, the party's medical expert was able to estimate that Tut-ankh-Amen's age when he died had been eighteen.

This would be the end of the story of the young king and his treasure if it were not for what became known in the press as "The Curse of the Pharaohs." Shortly after the discovery of the magnificent tomb was announced, the archaeologists natu-

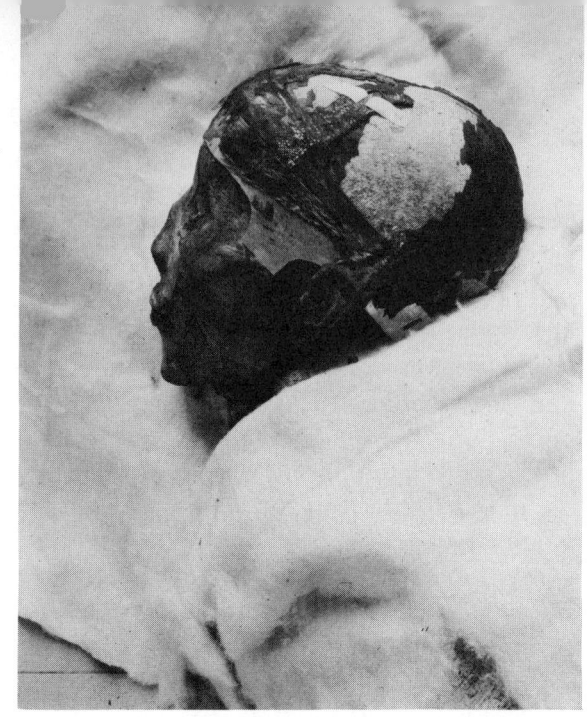

Head of Tut-ankh-Amen, side view

rally began to receive hundreds of letters and not all of them were favorable. There were some persons who declared that the archaeologists were merely grave-robbers themselves, "disturbing the sleep of the dead." The mixture of curiosity and horrified fascination that human beings often feel toward mummies in general was certainly made more intense by the fabulous treasure that was discovered and by the publicity given the whole affair. Thus when newspapers began running headlines like "Revenge of the Pharaohs Strikes Again" there were many who were willing to listen.

It is now very difficult to pin down the exact way in which the rumors about mysterious deaths got started. Probably the first event in the chain was the death of Carnarvon in April, 1923, of blood poisoning following an insect bite. However,

THE YOUNG KING'S TREASURE

"The Curse" really began to attract attention in the 1930's, when the number of "victims" was rising from the teens into the twenties. It was claimed that anyone who had anything to do with the opening of Tut-ankh-Amen's tomb was likely to meet a mysterious end. Victim Number Nineteen was supposed to have been Lord Westbury, who committed suicide by jumping from a seventh-floor window. His connection with The Curse was through his son, who had at one time been Howard Carter's secretary, and who had been found dead a few months before, although he had been thought to be in perfect health. Number Twenty was Archibald Douglas Reid, who was about to take an X-ray photograph of a mummy when he "dropped dead." Next came Arthur Weigall, a well-known Egyptologist who died of a fever. Other victims were Carter's partner A. C. Mace, Carnarvon's half brother (a suicide), and Carnarvon's daughter Elizabeth, who also died of an insect bite. The last was almost too much like a horror film. It raised up the image of swarms of tiny insects, each one zeroing in with deadly accuracy on the families and associates of those who dared disturb the tomb. Some may have recalled the plague of gnats that was sent upon the Egyptians by Moses, according to Exodus (8:6). It seemed that the capstone was put on the story by a report of the mysterious death of a man named Carter in the United States. Was The Curse now stalking Howard Carter, the only major investigator of the tomb now left alive? Apparently not. Carter lived a normally healthy life untroubled by disasters and died in 1939 at the age of sixty-six.

While it is amusing and exciting for everyone, except the probable victims, to believe in the power of ancient curses, the idea is not supported by facts. In 1933 a German archaeologist, Georg Steindorff, decided that the affair had gone far enough. He did a little research into the backgrounds of some of those who had died and discovered that several, such as Lord Westbury and his son, had had no part whatsoever in the actual opening of the tomb or in the study of the mummy. Furthermore, there was no connection or family relationship between the dead American named Carter and the British archaeologist.

Steindorff also pointed out that no evidence had ever been found to back up the wild rumors about the deadly nature of the tomb itself. Although the Egyptian architects had certainly gone to much trouble to mislead, hinder, and sometimes even entrap possible tomb robbers, this particular tomb at least had been carefully tested before it was entered. Thus the scientists could say for certain that no poisonous gases or disease-producing bacteria had built up in the tomb over the centuries. The tests, although not performed with such a far-fetched possibility in mind, had also shown that no deadly substance such as anthrax dust had been left to infect intruders. This last had been one of the most persistent rumors about the tomb, in spite of the fact that none of the "victims" had died of the disease called anthrax.

The most telling argument of all, however, the one that shows how large a part imagination had played in the tales of The Curse, was simply this: *There was no curse.* No papyrus scroll or wall inscription calls down death and misfortune on those who disturb the pharaoh's rest. The whole tone of The Book of the Dead and similar writings is one of reverence and hope for a better life. Requests that the reader pray for the dead person's soul are frequent; horrible curses do not appear at all.

Yet even now the human taste for marvels will not let the legend alone. On February 6, 1972, newspapers reported the death, of a brain hemorrhage, of Dr. Gamal Mehrez, Director-General of the Antiquities Department of the Egyptian Museum. The death occurred while experts were packing some of the priceless objects taken from the tomb of Tut-ankh-Amen for shipment to a loan exhibition at the British Museum. And although his colleagues denied Dr. Mehrez had taken any active part in the transfer and pointed out that the two men who *had* done so were alive and well, the headlines came out just the same. "Pharaoh's Curse: Another Victim?" It seems that after nearly fifty years the story has simply become too good to forget.

V
Chieftains and Headhunters

Mummies have been found in one form or another on every inhabited continent. But the methods and sometimes the intentions of those who made them (when they were made on purpose) have differed greatly from one time and place to another. There can be little doubt that the idea of preserving the dead was present among many of the native American peoples, but just how widespread the practice was and exactly how mummification was supposed to benefit the dead or the living is now a matter for guesswork. Not even the greatest of the American mummy-makers (the Incas, of whom we shall hear more in the next chapter) left us a Book of the Dead to tell us in detail how they saw the next world. Yet mummified bodies, or in one case, parts of bodies, have been found repeatedly in scattered places in the Americas.

Some of the best American mummies came from Alaska. The fact that the people of the Aleutian Islands treated their dead in this way was unknown until about a hundred years ago. Then, in 1874, an expedition sent out by the Alaska Commercial Company accidentally discovered a cave on Kagamil Island that reportedly contained thirteen mummies. In the same year, five mummies were found in an unnamed location and brought to San Francisco by Captain E. Hennig. Unfortunately, however, they were not given expert attention and soon were destroyed by a combination of poor handling and the warm climate.

For the next several decades a number of tall tales about mummies made the rounds of the Alaskan frontier. There was rumored to be a certain Island of the Four Mountains where the mummy caves were packed as thick as the cells in a beehive. Someone always knew an old native guide who claimed to have been there, or else a frontiersman who had set off for the place, never to return. It was said to be very unlucky to disturb the mummies or even to look for them. Still, every once in a while some trapper or miner would say he had stumbled on a mummy cave and lived to tell about it.

If these tales were usually ignored by archaeologists and others who were seriously interested in mummies, it is not too surprising. The unknown Alaskan wilderness spawned all sorts of strange stories and it was often hard to tell the false from the true. One of the liveliest of these stories concerned our friend the woolly mammoth—but not in the form of a frozen carcass. In 1899 a man named Henry Tukeman published a piece in *McLure's Magazine* telling in vivid detail how, in the trackless wilderness, he had shot and killed the last of the living mammoths after an exciting and bloody chase. If the story had been true, it would have been a sad addition to the human race's bad record as a destroyer of other species. But it was a hoax, for a while a widely believed hoax, and it was just another reason why sensible people treated any tale from Alaska with considerable suspicion.

Yet the rumors persisted, and in the 1920's a young man named Harold McCracken persuaded the American Museum of Natural History to send him on an expedition to find out whether there was in fact any such place as the Island of the

Four Mountains, and if so, whether there were any mummies there. McCracken had very little to guide him in his search—nothing but a vague description of the island's general location and appearance, given to him by an aged Indian trapper who claimed to have been there. Yet something had convinced McCracken that the story might be true, and after all, those five mummies brought to San Francisco had been real enough.

As it turned out, McCracken was both lucky and persistent. After considerable delays caused by bad weather, lack of supplies, and balky equipment, he and his party anchored their ship off an island in the southern Aleutians that seemed to fit the description in every way. Excitedly, they went ashore and began searching for caves. But though the island abounded in rocky clefts that might have been called caves, not so much as a finger bone could be found in any of them. It was only by accident that a junior member of the expedition came upon the "cave" that held the secret of the Aleutian mummies. It was not a natural cave but an artificial one, a log structure ten feet long buried under two to three feet of earth and sod.

When the logs had been carefully removed, the explorers found a layer of coarse grass matting below. Next came a layer of tanned sealskins, then more logs, mats, and skins, and finally a layer of sea lion gut sewn together in sheets, an excellent form of waterproofing. Under all this were a number of canoe paddles, perhaps for the long voyage to the underworld, and stone lamps to light the way. Now at last the two burial compartments could be seen. One contained a single mummy while the other held several. The bodies lay with their knees drawn up and hands at their sides on some sort of baskets or trays made of wooden hoops and sinew ropes. They were dressed in sealskin parkas and cloth leggings, their heads covered by several warm hoods. With them were many kinds of possessions—harpoons, spear shafts, wooden shields, sewn skins, and very finely patterned grass fabrics. It seemed plain that the single body was that of some great chief or warrior and the explorers guessed that the other persons in the tomb, who included both children and adults, might be those of his servants or followers. All were clearly dressed in their best and the workmanship of some of the garments and the grass cloth was especially fine.

As to the mummies themselves, their condition was not so good as to bring a gleam to the eye of an archaeologist who had spent his professional life among the tombs of Egypt. Though the cold climate undoubtedly helped preserve them, they were not actually frozen, as the mammoths were. Therefore they had been exposed to some natural decay and damage from the weather. The faces were in many cases almost without features and there certainly was none of the lifelike indi-

A mummy from the Island of the Four Mountains

Mummy from the Island of the Four Mountains

viduality that can be seen in the best Egyptian specimens. Nevertheless, they were undoubtedly true mummies, and not mere skeletons. The general shape of the bodies was well preserved and when they were examined more carefully it became apparent that much care had been taken in making them. The fingernails had been removed, as had the viscera, which had been replaced with straw. The eyeballs had also been taken out and balls of brown clay put in their place.

Another interesting thing about McCracken's finds was in the nature of the materials used in the burial. The tomb was constructed of logs, yet today there are no trees growing within seven hundred miles of the Aleutian Island where they were found. Could the makers of the tomb have brought them all that distance, or did the bodies date from a period (presumably long gone) when the islands were forested? A material even more scarce than wood in the area was amber. Yet one of the mummies wore three beads made of a type of amber that is only found in distant Korea.

After McCracken's historic discoveries, other mummified bodies began to turn up in the far north with some regularity. They all followed the same general pattern. They were found sitting or lying with the knees drawn up in what is called the flexed position, and the viscera had been removed and replaced with straw or sometimes, reportedly, with fur. Some, for example the bodies from Kagamil Island, had apparently been suspended from pegs, perhaps in a cave, while others had been placed in artificial caves of logs and earth like the mummies on the Island of the Four Mountains. Still others had been made up into bundles tied with rope netting, or banked with rocks and covered with boards like a group of bodies discovered near Prince William Sound. In the last case the remains

The mummies found by Harold McCracken were contained in trays or baskets of sealskin suspended on wooden hoops

of spruce wood canoes up to twelve and a half feet long were discovered with the mummies. This was extremely interesting because the people of the area today make their canoes from skins rather than from wood.

All these facts raise the question of the age of the Alaskan finds. Since no articles of foreign make, such as woven cloth or metal tools, have been found at the burial sites, most archaeologists have agreed that the mummies were made before the arrival of the first white men in the area. (Russian traders began coming there for sealskins in the early 1700's.) However, "sometime before 1725" is hardly the kind of precise date we would like to have for these remarkable mummies, and other kinds of evidence are confusing. On the one hand, the people of the area have legends that tell about the time when the first mummies were made, a time that doesn't seem to them to have been too long ago. Yet some of the Aleuts deny that the mummies were made by their people at all. This denial might be of great interest if it were not for the fact that since the Aleuts became converted to the Russian Orthodox Church they may think they *ought not* to have anything to do with such a "pagan" practice as mummification. So we are left with several mysteries. If the Aleuts did not make the mummies, who did, and where did the people come from? And in either case, what happened to the people who made the wooden canoes, how did the large, heavy logs get to the treeless Aleutian Islands, and who brought three amber beads all the way from the Asian peninsula of Korea, over three thousand miles away? We have a great deal to learn about the history of the North Americans before we can answer these questions.

The Aleutians are by no means the only place where mummies have been found in North America, but unfortunately we know even less about why and how mummies were made on the rest of the continent. From the fact that most have been discovered in places that are naturally favorable to mummification, it might seem that these mummies were of the kind that happen accidentally. But so much of the native American way of life was deliberately destroyed by the white man that we may never know, now, whether the mummies that have been found are accidents or examples of a widespread custom.

The Mammoth Cave of Kentucky is one of the largest natural limestone caverns in the world. Even today, it has

Mummy bundles found on Kagamil Island in the Aleutians

Unwrapped mummy from Kagamil Island

never been fully explored, but more than 150 miles of underground galleries are known to exist. In addition to limestone, the caves contain a large proportion of niter (potassium nitrate), a substance that readily absorbs water from the air and thus creates a very dry atmosphere suitable for the making of mummies. In 1815 some bodies were found in the cave—witnesses do not say exactly how many. They were quite well dried and were discovered in a seated or squatting position inside recesses scooped in the surrounding niter. One of the mummies was examined with care and found to be wrapped in the following coverings: first a layer of deerskin with the hair still on, then scraped deerskin, then a loose-meshed cloth covered with large brown feathers, and then another layer of coarse cloth, probably linen. The witnesses disagreed somewhat on the exact order and composition of the wrappings, but it was clear that the body had been placed in the cave after death and that some effort had been made to protect it from damage. Although the discoverers made no effort to preserve the mummies, and it was of course to be several decades before photography was invented, we do have the further information that the viscera had not been removed and that there was no sign of the use of preservative chemicals other than the natural niter in the cave.

Two years later a similar body was found in a smaller cave of the same type, one that was "only" three-quarters of a mile long, according to the discoverers. Ten feet below the surface lay the mummy of a woman in a position and with wrappings much like those just described above. In this case there was another feature as well. The mummy was surrounded by a row of broad stones standing on their edges and a large, flat stone had been laid over the top like a lid. Inside the stone enclosure were beads, feathers, and pottery. Perhaps someday the unexplored part of the Kentucky caves will yield another such find and archaeologists will be able to study it in more detail.

In the meantime, we must make do with reports of scattered discoveries that are too often vague or incomplete. The Far West has been the site of some very remarkable mummies, from the time of the first settlers to the present. In the 1880's a mummy was found in a cave near Ft. Casper, Wyoming. The body was that of a man about fifty-five years old. He had been placed in a kneeling position, looking westward from the cave mouth, and with him were fragments of cotton cloth, a leather belt, bracelets, a bird-quill necklace, a bridle and saddle, and stone-pointed arrows. There were also some metal arrowheads and some brass wire, showing that the man must have died sometime after the first contacts with white traders since the native Americans did not produce their own metal. There was no evidence that any artificial means had been used to mummify the body, and its discoverer, James Lisle, suggested that it had simply dried out in the mountain air. Perhaps, however, there was more to it than that. Lisle did not give a detailed description of the cave where the mummy was found, but the county in which Ft. Casper is located is called Natrona and the State of Wyoming is a leading producer of the sodium salts that are found in natron, the chemical used by the ancient Egyptians so many thousands of years ago. If the presence of natron was partly responsible for the drying of the body, which was so complete that the body weighed only twenty-five pounds, we will never know whether the people who used the cave for burial did so deliberately or simply by accident.

In any case, there is something solemn and moving in the picture of a man gazing forever out over the beautiful land, looking westward away from the direction from which came the invading white man.

In 1963 Harold McCracken found a similar mummy in a Rocky Mountain cave and it will probably not be the last such find.

MUMMIES

Dried mummies have also been found in the southwestern United States, where the climate offers some of the same advantages as that of the Egyptian desert. Mummies from this area are always in the flexed position and made into bundles with fiber rope.

Some early sources would lead us to believe that mummification was even more common among the native Americans. The early Floridians are said to have dried the bodies before a fire, dressed them in their best clothes, and set them in caves. In Kentucky the procedure was supposed to be to fill the body with sand, wrap it in skins, and bury it in a cave or under the floor of a hut. The people of Virginia were reported to remove the viscera and use "special preservative oils," whatever those might be. The problem with all these tales is that they often come from strangers who may have misunderstood what they saw or heard. Though they show some interesting likenesses to kinds of mummification practiced in South America, as we shall see shortly, we may wonder why, if mummification was practiced so widely and carefully, we have not found more

American Indian mummy from the southwestern United States

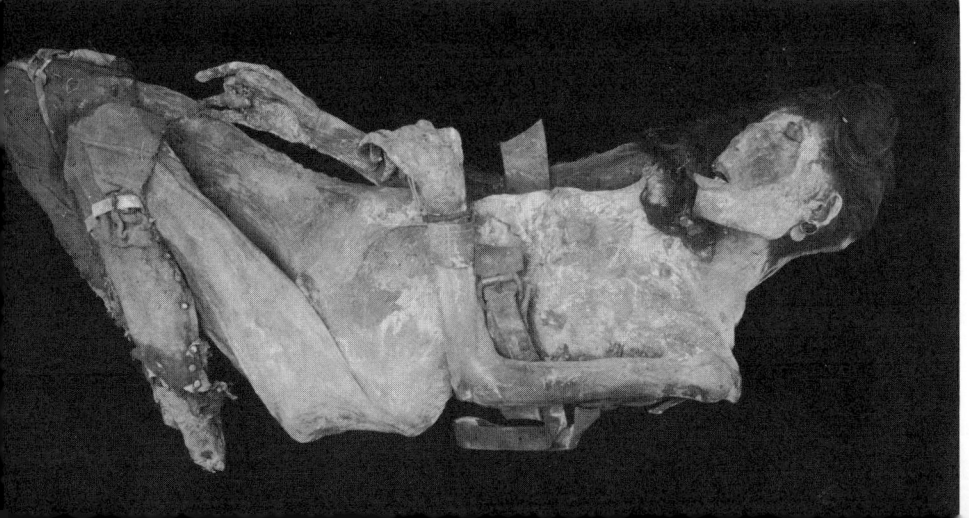

mummies in the areas mentioned. Yet the story of mummies in the Americas is far from finished. One of its strangest chapters takes place in a region that is still as little known as anywhere on earth, the headwaters of the Amazon River in South America.

The people who call themselves Jivaros live today in a vast area of rain forest north of the Marañon River and east of the Andes Mountains. They live by hunting, farming, fishing, and weaving. And they are headhunters. For no one knows how long, the Jivaros have been warriors who preserved the heads of their enemies by the so-called head-shrinking process. Their battles are fought mainly among themselves, but outsiders who disturb their territory also run the risk of becoming shrunken war souvenirs. That may explain why relatively little has been known about the Jivaros until recently, when they reportedly became somewhat less warlike.

The idea of not only preserving but "shrinking" human heads is not limited to the Jivaros; other peoples do the same thing in much the same way. But it is the Jivaros whose methods and way of life are best known, probably because they were the ones with whom the white men first came in contact.

When reports of the head-shrinking Jivaros reached Europe they caused quite a sensation. Since nothing at all was known of them beyond the few dried, wizened, orange-sized heads that had been brought out from the mysterious interior, many weird rumors soon began to circulate. The heads, it was said, were shrunk by magic and had uncanny powers. Their makers were evil and bloodthirsty people with unspeakable habits. In the nineteenth and early twentieth centuries, many horror stories and even some supposedly serious scientific books were based on fantastic tales about the Jivaros.

As one might guess from what we have already learned about mummies, the truth was less sensational but equally interesting. The Jivaros regard the shrunken heads as a special sort of trophy. Most, but not all, are the heads of those defeated in war. Others are those of personal enemies killed for revenge. In either case, the man who does the killing is not thought of as particularly brave or admirable. In fact, he is treated in many ways as if he had come down with a dangerous disease, which may be caught by everyone else unless something is done to prevent it. The man who has taken a head is made to stay outside the village for a certain time while he is purified with strong tobacco juice. A skeleton is also painted on his body, as if to convince the spirit world that he is already dead. This seems a strange custom, and the procedure for shrinking the head seems even stranger.

On the first day of the ceremony, at the same time that the murderer is being purified, the "shrinking" of the head is begun. The scalp is cut off and the rest of the head is carefully flayed—that is, the skin is detached from the skull—and the skull is removed through the neck. The village headman then dips the skin three times in boiling water and finally leaves it to boil for a considerable period. Some of those who have seen the ceremony claim that the liquid is not boiling water but the juice of a plant called *huito*. When the skin is taken out of its bath it is hung up on a spear shaft until the next day.

In the second part of the "shrinking" the hair is tightly tied with vines and the lips, eyelids, and neck opening are sewn up. Through the opening at the top the head is then filled with hot sand, which is changed whenever it begins to cool. The outside of the head is held against hot stones. Each part of the process is accompanied by an appropriate song. *"Ao apainaue, ao apainaue,"* sing the workers. "He is sewing, he is sewing." *"We yeyakum chumbiale."* "I am pouring sand." The effect of this treatment is, first, to melt out the fat beneath the skin, one of the earliest parts to decay. The heat also causes the skin to shrink. One may see the same thing happen when a piece of bacon is fried.

Shrunken heads of the Jivaro Indians

At the end of the hot-sand-and-stone treatment, the now darkened and shrunken skin is carefully pushed and prodded into its original shape. When the head, or *tsantsa,* as it is now called, has been completely treated, a triumphant procession carries it into the village, carefully covered. A celebration called the *wambo* follows, during which there is much dancing and drinking. Only after the *wambo* is over may the *tsantsa* be seen uncovered.

When we think about the Jivaran *tsantsa* ceremony, we see one enormous, obvious difference from all the other kinds of man-made mummies we have met so far: no one *wants* to become a *tsantsa*. In Egypt, the rich man used his wealth to pay for a better mummy. In the Aleutians and probably also in the rest of North America, only the greatest chiefs or warriors were given the furs and feathers and skins that preserved them in the burial caves. The Peruvians, too, as we shall see in the next chapter, mummified their dead as a sign of love and respect. In the case of the *tsantsa,* however, the main motive looks more like fear than devotion. In fact, the Jivaros' reason for making *tsantsas* seems like a combination of revenge and self-defense.

Like many other peoples, the Jivaros believe in magic and spirits. There are sorcerers among them who are supposed to have a special knowledge of such things, but in their view every man's spirit is a powerful and dangerous force. For this reason, when a man kills another man in war or in a quarrel, he is putting himself in grave peril. The *tsantsa* is made, not to honor the courage of the dead enemy as some have said, but *to defeat his magic.* The purpose is to shut him up inside his own head, one might say. That is why the lips and eyes are so carefully sewn shut. The dead man must not be able to curse his killer or look at him with the "evil eye." To the Jivaros, the head of an enemy is something like a bomb that may go off at any moment. It must not be brought into a village until it has been made harmless.

Given the Jivaran belief in magic and sorcery, the custom is perfectly logical. The only amazing thing is how well the procedure for shrinking a head has been made to work. The Amazon basin is one of the worst places in the world for preserving anything because it is damp and warm and therefore full of insects and bacteria. Some scientists think that there must be some important part of the process that we do not know about (perhaps the use of the mysterious *huito* juice) that accounts for the fact that the *tsantsas* seem to resist decay so well. Whether or not this is so, it is clear that the *tsantsas* provide one of the weirdest and most unusual aspects of the history of mummification.

VI
Peasants and Palace-Dwellers

From about A.D. 1200 to the time of the Spanish Conquest of the New World, parts of present-day Ecuador and Peru, Bolivia and Chile were the home of a great empire whose ruler called himself the Inca. When Pizarro and his men reached the capital city of Cuzco in 1533, they found a people whose way of life was in many ways as complex, varied, and interesting as that of any of the ancient kingdoms such as Egypt and Babylon, or even of Pizarro's own land of Spain. In their mountainous coastal empire the Incas had built great cities of stone, roads, temples, and palaces. Their carvings and pottery were beautiful and colorful, their metalwork was of the finest and their weaving was perhaps the best the world has ever seen. Like the Egyptians, the Inca people had a complicated religion in which the Inca, as ruler, was believed to be the earthly representative of the many gods. And, also like the Egyptians, the Incas mummified their dead.

Few of the arts and customs of the Incas were to last very long after the arrival of the Europeans, however. The empire fell to Pizarro and his tiny band of followers almost at once, its defeat hastened by disagreements among the ruling families.

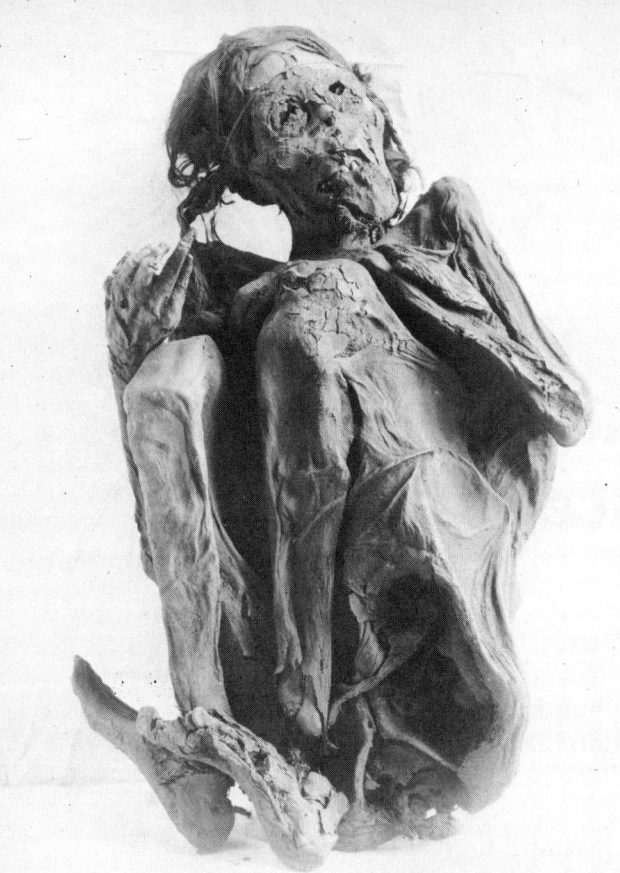

Mummy from Cuzco, Peru

Then followed a period in which the conquerors deliberately destroyed many objects of the greatest importance because they were "pagan," that is, part of a religion other than Christianity. Further damage was done through the looting of boatloads of artistic and historical treasures that happened to be made of gold and silver. The final blow to Inca life was given by the new foreign governors when they forbade the people to practice their own religious customs so that, in the absence of written records, the purpose, history, and meaning of many things were forgotten forever.

The Spanish conquerors were so anxious to take the Incas' gold and give them the Christian religion that there were many important facts about the Inca people that they apparently never bothered to find out. For example, they did report that it was the custom to mummify the Inca and his immediate family but they never suspected how widespread the practice really was. From what later archaeologists have been able to learn, the Incas, and the other Peruvian peoples who had been conquered and absorbed by them, were perhaps the only ones in history to mummify all their dead rather than just the nobles and those others who could afford it. Naturally, the style of burial for the common people was less extravagant than that of the Incas in their palaces. Yet, at least in certain times and places, even the poorest peasant apparently had his body preserved for the life after death.

We saw how the Egyptian tombs were arranged so that the pharaoh might live as royally in the Kingdom of the Dead as he had in the land of the living. The Inca rulers outdid even the Egyptians in this respect. When an Inca died, his body was carefully dried—by what method we do not really know—clothed in its magnificent imperial robes, and seated on a throne in his own palace. From that time on the palace was used only for the service of the dead Inca. His successor had to build an entirely new one, which would in turn become his permanent home when he died.

During a period of at least a year after his death, the dead Inca was treated as nearly as possible as if he were still alive. Servants brought him food in golden dishes, carried him to worship the gods, and even spoke to him. Members of the imperial family visited him, and he was taken from his palace to witness important events and festivals. Dramatic dances were performed before him showing the achievements of his reign. This cult of the dead emperor was called *panaca*. It not only expressed a religious belief in the life after death but also strengthened the rule of the royal family. The living Inca could point to the approving presence of his ancestors on all state occasions, so that his authority seemed to run in an unbroken line from the past to the present.

It is not clear exactly how long the dead Inca was waited upon as if alive. Certainly it was beyond even the wealth of the royal family to maintain as many separate imperial households as there had been ruling Incas. At some point, perhaps after the official year of mourning, perhaps after a longer period, the royal mummies were gathered together in a great hall, each

Mummy from Arica, Peru

sitting on his throne with his hands crossed over his chest.

When the Spaniards came, most of the royal mummies were hidden away to keep them from being destroyed as "pagan idols." However, Pizarro discovered the hiding place and burned all the mummies, to the great anguish of the people. So keen was the devotion they felt for the dead rulers that the royal ashes were stolen and revered as before. Even this was forbidden, however, and the ashes were eventually recaptured and "properly" buried. One of the mummies destroyed at this time is supposed to have been that of the Inca Viracocha, who died in the early part of the fifteenth century, thus giving us an idea of how long these mummies may have lasted.

Elsewhere in the former empire are found elaborate tombs in the form of earthen mounds entered by galleries at right angles to each other. There the mummies sat or stood, surrounded by all sorts of clothing, household objects, and valuables as well as the mummies of their families and servants. At least so tradition says. In the tombs of the nobles, but apparently not in other tombs, there was usually a carved figure known as the *huaoqui*. This figure served much the same purpose as the Egyptian *ushabti*. It was the dead person's "spirit brother," in which his luck was embodied. If anything should happen to the mummy, the *huaoqui* had the power to take its place in the afterlife. As far as this author knows, no complete tomb of that sort has been discovered and explored in modern times. Still, we may hope that such a find may be made someday. It was only in 1911 that an entire Inca fortress was first discovered on the high slopes of the Andes—the city of Machu Picchu.

Strangely enough, it is the burial places of more or less ordinary people that have given us our best information about Peruvian mummies. Like the Egyptians, the Peruvians also brought their dead together in necropolises, or cities of the dead.

A landward view of the rocky plateau of Ancón

Not all the Peruvian necropolises are alike, by any means, and unfortunately there is not enough information at present to show clearly which styles belong to which periods or groups of peoples. Unlike Egyptian history, Peruvian history cannot yet be divided into neat slices such as dynasties, each with its particular tomb style and method of mummification.

In some areas one finds tombs made of unbaked brick with sloping sides and flat tops, about twenty or thirty feet high. These are called *chulpas.* A simpler kind of tomb has just one square underground chamber in which up to a dozen mummies may be found sitting in a sharply flexed position. An odd feature of some of these finds is that the mummies have had a series of holes made in the backs of their heads. These holes are not injuries to the living person, but were apparently made

after death. We do not know exactly what they were for, although a good guess might be that they were made either to let the "spirit" escape from the skull at the time of death or else to let it get back in at some future time when the body was to be revived. The latter possibility is not so different from Christian and Jewish ideas about the Day of Judgment, when "the dead shall be raised incorruptible" (I Corinthians 15:52). In the Jewish and Christian tradition it is forbidden to try to make the body actually incorruptible (undecaying), but among the Peruvians it plainly was not.

One of the most interesting Peruvian necropolises was first explored in 1875. The tomb city is at Ancón, a bay on the coast of Peru about twenty-four miles north of the city of Callao. It is a barren, rocky landscape where low spurs of the

A deep grave shaft at Ancón, in which false-headed mummies were found

nearby mountains run down into the sea and the climate is almost rainless. Because Ancón was in a remote region, far from major cities, and not on the main route to anywhere, it had apparently been overlooked by the Spanish conquerors in their search for plunder. Though the tombs showed traces of some disturbance in later times, they were still largely untouched. The tomb robbers in this case had probably been attracted by tales of the necropolis that began to filter out during the building of a railway line from Lima which passed close to Ancón. However, the earliest reference to Ancón as a necropolis comes from the first part of the nineteenth century, when whole boatloads of mummies were used as ballast in ships sailing for Europe. There is little way of telling how many were carried away in this manner, so that the total original size of the necropolis remains unknown.

PEASANTS AND PALACE-DWELLERS

From the sea, the view of Ancón is not very exciting. The tombs were largely unmarked except by low stone walls that blend into the rocky landscape. The graves themselves were pits or shafts dug into the ground, as much as eighteen to twenty feet deep. The entrances had been so carefully covered over that the only way to find them was by prodding the earth with a stick or rod until empty spots were found, or else by looking for faint differences in the gravel that lay on the surface.

When the tombs were opened, the bodies were found in

Cross-sectional views of several styles of grave (Ancón)

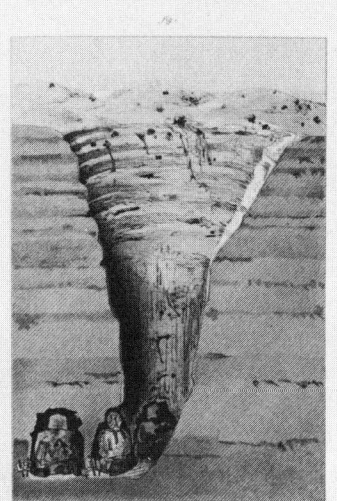

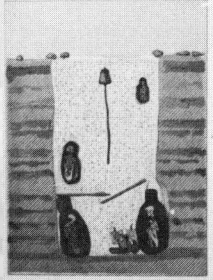

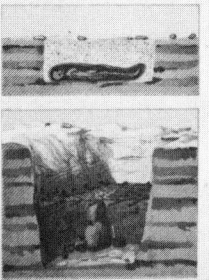

chambers at the foot of the shafts. Some tombs contained several mummies, some only one. It was also clear that in some cases all the mummies had been put into the tomb at more or less the same period, while in others the tomb had been reopened again and again to add new occupants, perhaps members of the same family. Each mummy was found in the now familiar sitting posture with knees drawn up. Wrappings such as cloth, seaweed, leaves, grass matting, and furs had been used to make each mummy into a triangular bundle laced with rope. Sometimes the bodies were also covered over with enormous earthenware jars.

The truly extraordinary thing about the mummies of Ancón, however, was the appearance of the mummy bundles. Many of the mummies were equipped with a sort of false head with a face and eyes that stared out into the darkness of the tomb. These heads were made rather like cushions, being stuffed balls of cloth. They were usually painted red and their expressions were more alert and friendly than frightening. Noses were often made of carved wood sewn onto the cloth, while the eyes were of shells, white bark, or, in a few cases, silver. Hair was either real or made of plant fiber, and there were headdresses of feathers, corncobs, pieces of metal, and richly woven bands. The height of the mummy packs with their false heads was sometimes as much as five feet. In the dimly lit burial chambers, they must have looked to the explorers like a strange council of grinning ghosts sitting cross-legged in a centuries-long conversation.

What was the purpose of this remarkable feature of the Ancón mummies? We cannot know for certain until much more has been unravelled from the tangle of Peruvian history. However, we may be sure that the heads were in some sense "spirit heads." Perhaps they kept watch on the outer world while the mummy dreamed in the inner one. Perhaps they were the eyes of the spirit in the land of the dead. Since there

Large mummy with false head

Front and back views of the head of the same mummy, unwrapped

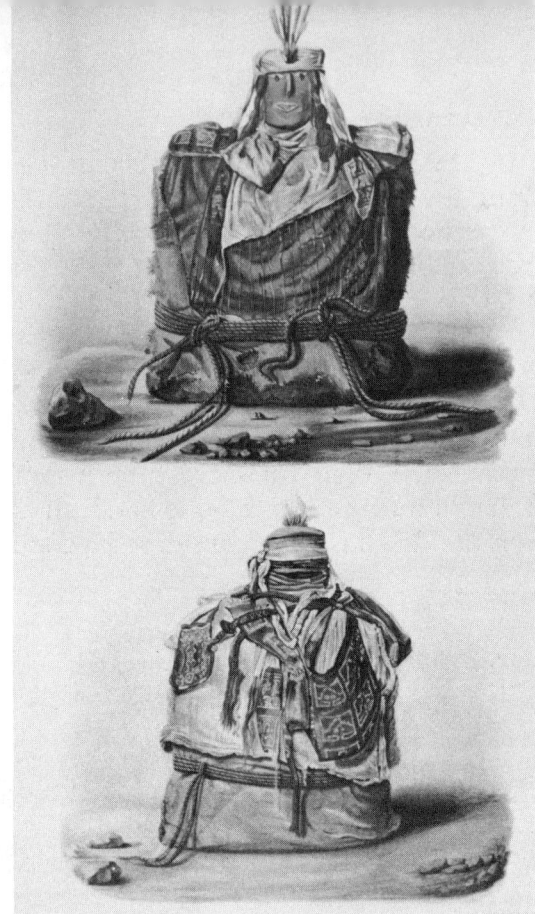

Two mummies from one grave

is no sign that the heads were meant to resemble individual persons, it was probably *what* they were rather than *who* they were that was important. They may even have been intended to frighten away evil demons who might try to attack the spirit. No doubt there are other possibilities as well. If we only knew more about what the Peruvian people believed about the afterworld we might have the answer.

One clue is in the goods that are found in the Ancón graves. Given the differences in the two cultures, they are very much like those used by the Egyptians. That is, the graves simply provide everything the occupants might need in order to live the same life in the next world that they had lived in this one. There are baskets of cotton for spinning, nets for fishing, containers of dried beans and fruit, and foodstuffs such as maize, yucca, and crayfish. The mummies of children were often provided with toys. Various kinds of mummified animals have also been found in the tombs. The dog, the guinea pig, the parrot, the frog, and the dove are the most common, and they raise an interesting question. Were these creatures meant to be food, pets, or religious offerings? On the one hand, all of them can be eaten. Even the dog has been considered a good

Many styles of false heads

meal in the Americas. On the other hand, it might be more reasonable to preserve foods in cooked form rather than as whole animals. But if the animals mentioned are not intended for food, what are they? Frogs hardly seem like anyone's first choice for a pet, and we know of no gods to whom the various creatures were especially sacred, particularly not the frog and the guinea pig.

Another mystery of the Ancón graves is the large number of odd but attractive objects that serve no apparent useful purpose. There are rods and crosses made of sticks, wound with colored thread, decorative bits of tufted reed, and objects best described as tablets, either woven or painted with certain designs. Often these things are found bundled together or stuck in the sand beside the mummies. No one really knows what they mean. They may be some sort of amulet of the kind the Egyptians used to protect the mummy, or they may have an unknown religious meaning. Ancón is full of mysteries that only become more puzzling as we look at the contrast formed by other Peruvian necropolises.

At Paracas, for example, the mummies were buried in the same general manner, but do not have false heads. Instead, they were provided with a spectacular supply of woven goods and clothing made of cotton or llama hair all in vivid colors and fine designs. Belts, turbans, ponchos, and shawls were most common. Sometimes the clothing was made in miniature, as if it were only meant to symbolize the garments worn by the spirit. However, one single length of cloth from Paracas measured 11-1/4 feet by 87-1/2 feet and others were nearly as large. This is a staggering size for cloth woven by hand. It must have meant that several women devoted not months but years to the project, using about two hundred miles of two-ply yarn. Add to this the fact that modern experts have judged Peruvian weaving to be the finest in the world in terms of evenness of thread and denseness of weave, and we begin to see how

Two simple mummies. Notice the resemblance of the mummy pack on the left to the one from Kagamil Island in the Aleutians

important the mummies were to the people who made them.

To take just one example of the goods provided for those entombed at Paracas, the so-called "Mummy 49" had eleven big mantles, twenty ponchos and shirts, eleven skirts, six turbans, five belts, and twenty-six pieces of cloth, one of which was the very large one mentioned above. There were in this tomb also twelve pieces of sheet gold, a shell necklace, a fox skin, a fan, a wooden baton, a stone-headed club, a wooden knife handle, and a sling. Considering that this man was apparently not an emperor or even a high-ranking noble, but only a local leader of some sort, it is clear that the arrangements for a royal mummy must have been magnificent indeed.

We have talked a good deal about the funeral arrangements made for the Peruvian mummies, but not very much about how the mummies themselves were made and what they looked like. To answer the last question, here is a description written by a Captain Basil Hall, who visited Peru in 1824.

> I went this morning to the palace to breakfast with the Protector, and to see a curious mummy or preserved figure, which had been brought the day before from a Peruvian village to the northward of Lima. The figure was that of a man seated on the ground, with the knees almost touching his chin, the elbows pressed to the sides, and the hands clasping his cheek bones. The mouth was half open, exposing a double row of fine teeth. The body, though shrivelled up in a remarkable manner, had all the appearance of a man, the skin being entire, except on one shoulder ...
>
> ... There was [found] seated near the same spot a female figure with a child in her arms. The female had crumbled into dust on exposure to the air; but the child, which was shown to us, was entire. It was wrapped in a cotton cloth woven very neatly, and composed of a variety of brilliant colors and quite fresh. Parts of the clothes also which the female figure had worn were equally perfect, and the fibres quite strong. The bodies were dug up in a part of the country where rain never falls, and where the sand, consequently, is so perfectly dry as to cause an absorption of moisture so rapid that putrefaction [decay] does not take place.*

*Pettigrew, T. J., *A History of Egyptian Mummies.* London: Longmans, 1834.

PEASANTS AND PALACE-DWELLERS

It is likely that Captain Hall's statement about how the mummies were made is largely correct. As we saw with the earliest Egyptian examples, very dry sand is an excellent place for mummification, and the climate of much of Peru is extremely dry, although much colder than that of Egypt. Probably the first Peruvian mummies were completely natural, and from them the people learned to mummify the dead by drying. In some cases, mummies have reportedly been found that showed evidence of other methods of preservation, such as removal of the viscera. In at least one report the bodies were smoked as well, and some of the large masses of muscle were removed. However, these are only unusual cases, even if true. It may be that the Peruvians were only just beginning to experiment with new and better methods of preservation at the time of the Spanish Conquest, or perhaps mummification was always done in different ways in different regions.

Certainly it would be fascinating to know exactly, step by step, how the Inca emperors were mummified. Yet it may be

Copper Man

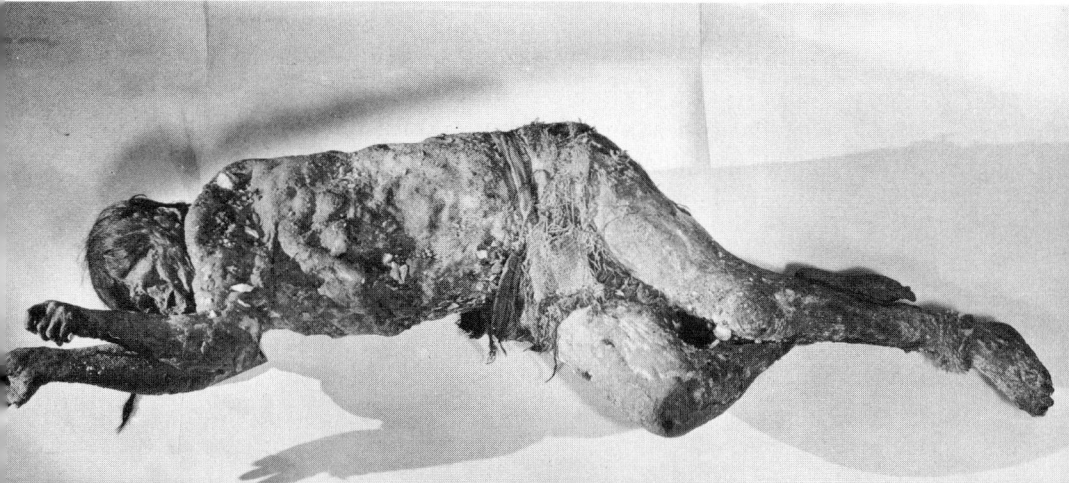

that the Incas, unlike the Egyptians, did not try to improve on the natural drying effect of the local climate.

In 1905 a party of explorers discovered a preserved body high in the Andes near Antofagasta, Chile. Apparently dating from before the Spanish Conquest, the body was that of a copper miner who had been killed in a cave-in. The man—or, it may have been, the woman—lay just as he had fallen, with a collection of tools nearby. The dry air of those high altitudes, coupled with the action of copper salts from the mine, had mummified the Copper Man as perfectly as the most carefully tended Inca, and there he had lain for upwards of four centuries.

VII
Islands and Outbacks

Up to this point, we have looked at cases of human mummification on three continents and in at least two very highly developed civilizations. Now we must take a rather rapid round-the-world tour of several other places where mummies are found, although in many cases we shall have to work with guesses about the why and how of mummification, rather than with definite facts. That is because the peoples who made these mummies range from some of the most primitive in the world to a group of islanders who died out more than four hundred years ago, and because many of them live in places that are almost as little known as the Amazon basin of the Jivaros.

The islands of the southern Pacific Ocean, most of which were first seen by Europeans only about two hundred years ago, are the source of many reports of mummification, though it is not always possible to know how accurate they are. In Tahiti, for example, the famous voyager Captain Cook observed that the Polynesian inhabitants preserved the bodies of their chiefs, at least for some time after death. The body was placed on a bier in the sun and the drying process was aided by pressing in order to remove the fluids. Later the mummy was anointed with oils (what kind of oils is not stated) and the viscera were removed and replaced with cloths soaked in oil. The mummy was then placed in a sitting position and clothed in its best, while offerings were made to the departed spirit. It is clear, however, that the process used here did not keep the mummy from decaying eventually, because it is stated that the skull was kept permanently in a sacred place. This detail fits in well with the fact that the head was regarded as extremely sacred all over Polynesia. There were many magical rules, or *tabus,* about the head that were rigidly followed by everyone from kings to common people. Another reasonable thing about the report, which has apparently never been confirmed by the discovery of any actual mummies, is the way it implies that the mummies did eventually decay. The island of Tahiti is neither a sandy desert, a rainless coastland, nor a frozen wasteland such as we have seen may be favorable for producing mummies. It does not even have caves rich in niter. Instead, it has a warm, balmy climate that would surely make it difficult, if not impossible, to preserve bodies permanently by the rather simple methods described.

Far, far to the south and west of Tahiti, which is itself a long way below the equator, are the two large and several smaller islands that make up New Zealand. The native inhabitants of New Zealand are called Maoris (pronounced *Mowrees*) and their way of life is one of the most interesting in the world, simply because it is least like the complicated, industrial existence we call modern. To visit the Maoris, or many of the other inhabitants of the Pacific islands, is like going back in a time machine to a period when all of our ancestors lived by hunting game and gathering foods—a time when there were no domestic animals but the dog and tools and weapons were made only of wood or stone.

The reports of the earliest students of Maori life make it

clear that several methods of disposing of the dead were used by the Maoris before the coming of the white man. Some groups burned the bodies, some buried them, and some even put the dead inside the hollow trunks of trees. There was quite a lot of argument about which groups used which methods of burial, and also about scattered reports that mummification was also practiced in some cases. In 1916–17 several learned members of the Polynesian Society engaged in an angry debate on the subject, basing their opposing points of view on the question of whether there were or were not genuine Maori mummies to be found in the local museums. The amusing thing about the dispute is that neither side paid a great deal of attention to a paper by another anthropologist *who was himself a Maori,* a paper that described the Maori mummies in some detail and appeared in the same issue of the *Polynesian Society Journal* as did the learned debate.

The name of the paper's author was Hare Hongi. He testified not only that mummies *were* made by the Maori, but that he had actually seen them himself as a child. According to Mr. Hongi's account, those who were mummified were usually chiefs or members of important families. His own sister had died as a young woman and he remembered paying visits to her mummy and noting that it was still perfectly recognizable.

When it was decided to make a mummy, the first step was to build a small house decorated with carvings, inside an enclosure to whose posts were tied bunches of feathers. An oven pit was made in the center of the house and the body was seated over it. Thus the body was dried and smoked at the same time. Openings were also made in the body so that its fluids could drain out. The brain was removed, though we are not told how, and the body was sometimes stuffed with tow or flax. An entirely different sort of preservation was practiced on the heads of important Maori men, which were dried, sewn up, and

A Maori mummy. Photo taken in 1893 of a mummy which probably came from a cave at Kawhia, South Island, New Zealand

smoked in order to preserve their magnificent tattoo patterns.

On Mangaia in the Cook Island group of Polynesia still another form of mummification is reported. After being sun-dried and treated with oils, the bodies were wrapped in cloth and taken to a sacred cave called Kauava. Some sources say these mummies were kept in wooden cases or coffins carved in human shape, rather like the Egyptian mummy cases, but there is disagreement about the truth of this. Certainly it would be unusual to find coffins of this kind in Polynesia.

Moving a little farther west in the Pacific, we find that in certain areas of Australia there have been scattered reports of the mummified remains of the native inhabitants, called aborigines. Little is known of these mummies, however, except that they always seem to be found in a flexed position rather than lying straight. It is not even certain whether they are artificial or natural.

In the area of the Torres Strait, the body of water that lies between northern Australia and southern New Guinea, there was found, in 1872, a very remarkable mummy which became known as the Lemaistre specimen after its discoverer. The body was standing upright in a cone-shaped native hut, supported by a sort of stretcher or framework. The head had been painted black and the body red, while the face was equipped with artificial eyes. There was an opening on the right side of the body, through which the viscera had apparently been re-

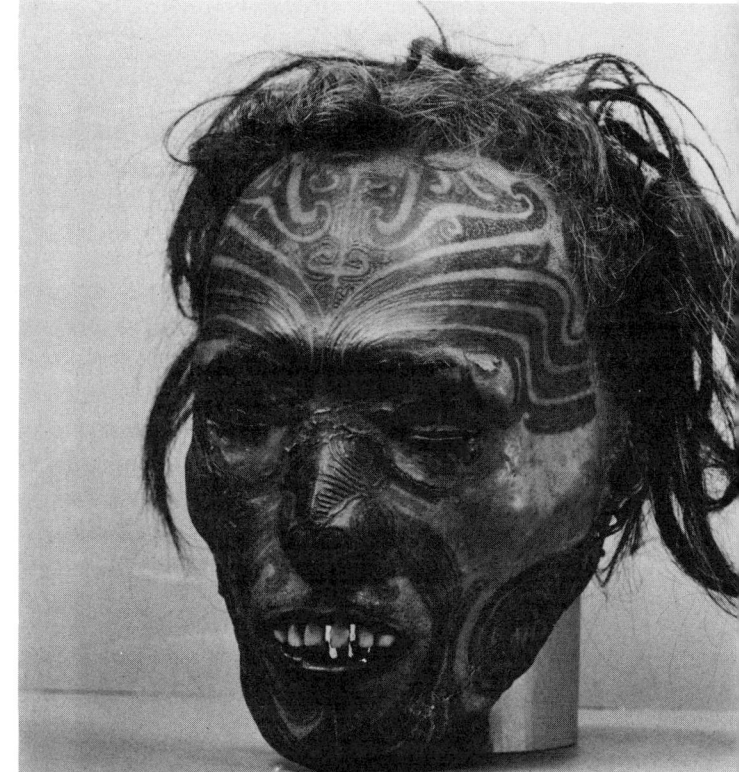

Maori smoked head, showing tattoo patterns

moved. Standing in the dim light of the hut, the red and black mummy with its staring eyes must have been an astonishing sight. It is likely that the Lemaistre mummy was made by the nearby Papuan people of New Guinea who are also known to preserve heads, which are dried and then decorated with features painted or modeled in clay.

In Indonesia in times past, the practice of mummification was quite widespread. Interestingly, it was often combined with a form of burial mentioned earlier as having been practiced among the Maoris. This was tree burial. Certain Indonesian peoples apparently preserved their dead by drying and/or smoking, after which the mummies were then placed inside hollow trees. Probably this custom was connected with religious ideas about trees and their spirits, since we know that tree-worship was once an important part of local life. However, it appears that this sort of mummification was only supposed to be temporary. Whether because the climate was so unfavorable for permanent preservation, or whether for some religious reason, the Indonesian mummies were eventually disposed of in a more usual way, by burial or burning.

The fact is that our information about mummies in these areas is confusing and incomplete. One reason is that the methods of mummification used were apparently much less highly developed, at least in many places, than they were in Egypt or Peru. A more important factor is the unfavorable climate. Finally, there is the fact that on many of the smaller islands the native way of life was all but swept away overnight by the coming of the white man. Unlike the North Americans, the Polynesians had nowhere to go in order to escape the newcomers, and those who did not die of the white man's unfamiliar diseases were quickly taught to forget or reject all they knew of their people's history and customs. This destruction was not quite total, but it was complete enough to explain why, in the absence of written records, we do not know more

Tree burial in Australia

than we do concerning treatment of dead bodies and beliefs about the afterlife. And finally, there is the fact that in Australia and Indonesia, at least, there are still large areas of land that are not thoroughly explored. The world's second, third, and sixth largest islands (New Guinea, Borneo, and Sumatra) are all to be found here, and they have a combined area of well over 760,000 square miles, mainly covered with high mountains and dense jungle. Large parts of the dry interior of Australia, usually called the outback, are equally little known and little traveled. It is at least conceivable that some tribe that mummifies its dead or some ancient mummy cave may still be discovered to tell us more about mummies of the Pacific.

Still another group of mummies is found halfway around the world, on the Canary Islands in the Atlantic Ocean off the coast of North Africa. The early history of the Canaries is mysterious, although they were mentioned by some of the later Greek and Roman writers. The original inhabitants, the Guanches, were not Africans, but little is known of their way of life because they died out in the early sixteenth century, following the fifteenth-century conquest of the islands by Norman, and later Spanish, colonists.

Legend insists that the Guanches were the last survivors of the people of the mythical kingdom of Atlantis, a vast continent that is supposed to have sunk into the Atlantic Ocean before the dawn of history. A more reasonable suggestion is that their ancestors arrived by boat from southern Europe in prehistoric times. They may even have been members of the group called Cro-Magnon men, the first "true men" who were ancestors of the modern Europeans. But wherever they came from, it is certain that the Guanches practiced mummification. Reports of this custom appear in the first European accounts of the islands. In 1526 one cave alone was found to hold three or four hundred mummies and the discoverers were told by their guides that only a small fraction of the caves had been found. Some of the mummies were found lying at full length, others standing upright, and a few even appeared to have been hung from pegs in the cave wall. In another early report the mummies were said to be very light, weighing no more than six or seven pounds each, while in 1762, a cave containing several mummies prompted one writer to remark that their well-preserved flesh was "as hard as wood." If this is so, then the Guanches must have been quite knowledgeable about mummification, a conclusion that is confirmed by the large numbers of mummies found by the first settlers.

The Baganda people of what is now the East African country of Uganda formerly practiced a very interesting and unusual form of mummification upon their kings and other members of the royal family. When a Baganda ruler died his death was kept secret from the people until the new king had secured his claim to the throne and assumed the symbols of power. The death of a ruler is always a time when the throne may be in danger from rivals or revolutionary factions, and that may have been the original reason why the news was not made public until the period of transition was over. If so, it would then be necessary to preserve the king's corpse in some way, however, for the people would expect the body to be on view, both so that they could pay their respects and so that all might know the king had died a natural death.

Accordingly, the body was eviscerated and the internal organs were preserved by washing in beer. The body also was washed in beer and was then tightly wrapped in bark cloth. The effect of this tight wrapping was heightened by pressing so that all the bodily fluids were removed and the flesh was at least partially preserved by drying. Finally the body was again wrapped in bark cloth and heavily smeared with butter (which might possibly have served to keep it flexible). At the end of the five months' official mourning period the body was laid in a grave inside a new hut, which was then entirely filled with bark cloth. The last duty of the mourners was to remove the center pole of the hut so that its conical roof settled down upon the body, making a very noticeable grave marker. This was not the last act in the history of the mummy, however. Months later a tunnel was cut into the burial hut and the king's jaw (some sources say the entire head) was carefully removed, cleaned, polished, and used to make an effigy or portrait of the dead king. From that point on, the most reverent attention was paid to the jaw (or head), which was believed to offer wise advice and decisions to the people. The mummified body, meanwhile, was largely ignored and the burial hut untended.

At this point it may be reasonable to ask, "Why have so many different peoples all over the world made mummies and why does it seem as if they were often made in much the same way? Did all the mummy-makers learn from each other, that is, from the Egyptians? Or did the idea of making mummies come up by itself in different places at different times?"

Some of these questions have relatively easy answers, some are harder to answer, and some really do not have definite answers at all. For example, it is quite easy to see that the mummies of North and South America all fall into the same general pattern. Whether the main reason for their preservation was the cold climate of Alaska, the niter-dried air of Mammoth Cave, or the rainless air of Peru, they are almost all found in caves or cavelike places such as hollow tombs built in the earth or made of logs. The mummies are usually lying or sitting in a flexed position rather than standing or lying straight. The custom of wrapping the mummy in many layers of cloth or skins is also characteristic of the Americas and the practice of making mummy bundles laced with rope is found in places as far apart as the Aleutians, the southwestern United States, and Peru.

These similarities seem quite reasonable when we understand that the peoples of the Americas apparently came to the New World from the same general area of Asia and by the same route—across the Bering Strait to Alaska. Thus although different groups made the journey at different times, it is probable that they all brought with them similar ideas about the life after death which sometimes, when conditions were favorable, developed into a desire to preserve the dead.

The case with the mummies of Polynesia, Indonesia, and Australia is more complicated. The peoples of these areas are separated from each other by ocean as well as by distance and it is hard to know how much communication there was among them, although the Polynesians probably voyaged eastward from Indonesia to reach their present homes. Furthermore, the ancient civilizations of Japan, China, and India certainly at various times brought their influences to parts of this vast collection of islands. Customs and ideas washed back and forth over it from the north and west, and perhaps also from the east, since it has now been shown that there was certainly some contact between Polynesia and South America before the time of the Spanish Conquest. But in spite of these conflicting influences, we can also see some similarities among the different types of Pacific mummies: the general absence of large quantities of grave goods or supplies to be used in the afterlife and the habit of "visiting" the mummy as if it were still alive, for example. The Pacific view of mummies seems to be more closely connected with the here-and-now than with the complicated world of the dead on which the Egyptians centered their thoughts. Some writers have remarked that the Egyptian people existed only to serve the dead, although that is something of an exaggeration. By contrast the mummified Polynesian chief and the Baganda ruler were expected to serve the living with their continued advice and support.

And yet, there are some interesting and disturbing ways in which the methods of mummification used in the South Pacific and elsewhere do resemble those of the Egyptians, particularly the Egyptians of Dynasty XXI. For example, during that period the epidermis (the outermost layer of skin) was generally removed from the body during the process of mummification. However, the Egyptians plainly went to some trouble to make sure the finger and toenails did not come off at the same time. So that the dead man would not have to face eternity without those important parts of his hands and feet, cuts were made around each finger and toe and the ends were fastened in place with string. Oddly enough, the Australian aborigines, the Guanches, and sometimes the Peruvians did exactly the same thing while the Papuan mummies of New Guinea show a strange reversal. In the latter case, cuts were also made around the fingers and toes, but the "thimbles" thus made were then pulled off rather than being carefully left in place. It is almost enough to make one think that the Papuans were acting out of a misunderstanding of the original method. Another point of resemblance is in the place chosen for the incision when the viscera were to be removed, a point that is often the same whether the mummy is from Egypt, the Canary Islands, or New Guinea.

Facts like these are hard to explain away, even though the vast distances and cultural differences involved make it unlikely that the Egyptians had any direct influence on, say, the early ancestors of the Polynesians and the Peruvians. The idea of Egyptian contact with the Canary Islands is not so far-fetched, however. The Egyptians certainly traveled widely along the coast of North Africa, both by land and by sea. The modern anthropologist and adventurer Thor Heyerdahl recently showed beyond doubt that the reed boats used by the Egyptians were quite able to make sea voyages many times longer than the hundred miles or so that separate the African coast from the nearest of the Canaries. And finally, what is

Human head, skull stuffed with fiber, mouth choked with clay and smoke-cured for preservation

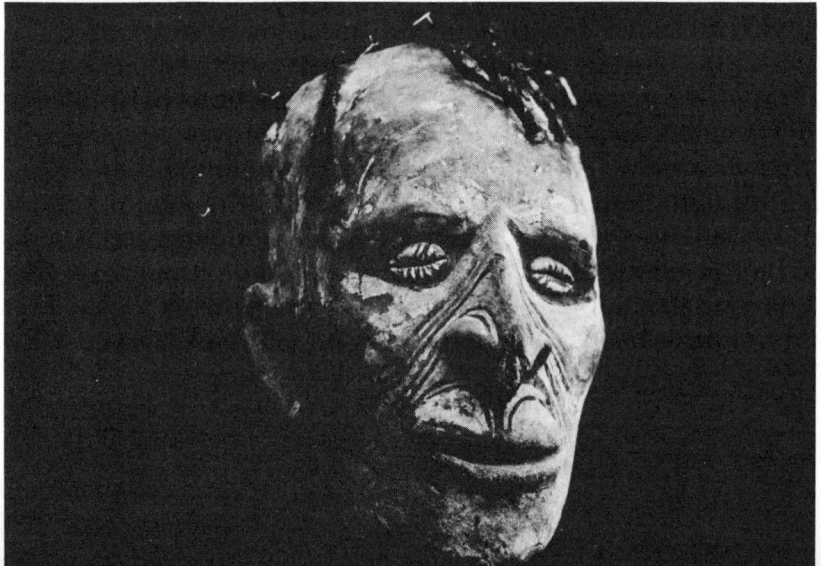

known of the Guanches' methods of mummification sounds a good deal more Egyptian than do most of the others we have mentioned. In addition to the treatment of the finger and toenails and the placing of the incision, some Guanche mummies also have sandy mud packed under the skin for the purpose of keeping the body's shape, exactly as it was done with Egyptian mummies of the twenty-first dynasty. Furthermore, some reports from the Canaries mentioned the finding of human-shaped or so-called anthropoid coffins made of wood. If the reports were correct, the coffins apparently proved more subject to decay than the mummies they contained, for few if any have lasted into the present. Yet that anthropoid coffins, so typical of the surrounding of the Egyptian mummy, should have been reported from the Canary Islands definitely lends weight to the idea that Egyptian influence was at work.

With regard to the Baganda, it is plain that their customs have much in common with those of the Pacific islanders, especially in the emphasis that is put on the head and the belief that through it, one may communicate with the spirit of the dead man. On the other hand, the fact that the Baganda live so much closer to Egypt than to the Pacific is sure to raise the question of whether the custom is one that has survived from a period when it might have been influenced by the mummy-makers of Egyptian dynastic times. Some writers on the subject have suggested that the wrapping of the body in bark cloth resembles the use of linen bandages in Egypt. However, the study of African history and culture was neglected too long for us to be able to say positively where or how the custom arose. There is really no proof that the Baganda did not invent their method of preserving the dead quite independently, without any direct outside influence.

VIII
Bodies in the Bogs

So far, all the mummies we have discussed have been made by one of two basic methods—freezing and drying—sometimes with the addition of chemicals to slow down the process of decay. It was another kind of mummification entirely that produced the remarkable mummies that have turned up from time to time in the bogs of northern Europe.

To understand what the *bog bodies* are and how they were made, it is useful to know something about the particular kind of bog where they occur. The word *bog* can of course mean any damp, soft, marshy place anywhere in the world. However, in the areas mentioned above, bogs are usually of the type known as peat bogs. That is because they are the home of several closely related small plants called peat mosses, and peat mosses have some interesting characteristics. First of all, although peat moss is very soggy and damp while it is growing, it can be used as fuel after it is dead. Layers and layers of it sink to the bottom of the bogs as the seasons go by and eventually they form a dark earthy-looking substance that has been burned in the fireplaces of northern Europe from earliest times to the present. But, like wood or coal or any other fuel of this sort, peat has to be dug or cut before it can be used. Old peat bogs, therefore, are often crisscrossed with peat diggings made after the bog filled up and became dry enough to work in. In modern times the bogs are often drained to make them available to the peat cutters. This explains why people have spent time digging up peat bogs, but it is another characteristic of peat moss that explains what the diggers have sometimes found.

When peat moss dies and decays in the water of a bog it releases certain acids into the water. These acids have much the same properties as tannin, a substance used in the tanning of leather. For this reason, any living thing that falls into a bog may be preserved by the bog water just as if it had been turned into leather.

There is another characteristic of bogs that has certainly played a role in the story of the bog bodies. Unless they have been drained or dried out, bogs are rather dangerous and, in the dark or fog, eerie places. A large bog may stretch away for miles in all directions—a flat, watery place where pools of shallow water alternate with greenish hummocks and perhaps a few low shrubs or reeds. Nothing is solid in a bog and nothing can be counted on to be what it seems. The careless person who tries to find his way over the bog will be lucky if he only lands up to his knees in water. The unlucky often discover that the bottom of the bog is as treacherous as the top. It is possible to become hopelessly stuck in the black ooze (that is the meaning of the expression "bogged down") and almost equally possible to sink right out of sight and drown. Thus it is not surprising that a few bodies should now and then turn up in the bogs.

Actually, the bogs of Scandinavia, Great Britain, Germany, Holland, and a few scattered areas elsewhere have yielded at least 690 bodies during the last few centuries, according to a study done recently in Germany. Records of such finds go back as far as the 1700's and we can only guess how many bog bodies appeared before that and how many finds were never reported. It was only natural that those who discovered the bodies were often scared out of their wits by what they saw. Some believed the bodies were the work of the Devil. Others were frightened of becoming involved in police investigations. This last may seem incredible, but the truth is that some bog bodies have been so perfectly mummified that one might indeed think the deaths had happened recently.

The facts show something very different and far more exciting. Though a few of the bog bodies are of modern date, including airmen and soldiers of the two World Wars, it has recently been established that a surprisingly large number are centuries old. The man who has done the most extensive and best-known work on the earlier bog bodies is Dr. P.V. Glob, the Director General of Denmark's Museums and Antiquities. His reports, descriptions, and conclusions have been the main source for the account of the most recent bog finds that follows.

The two most famous of the bog bodies are certainly the so-called Tollund Man and the Grauballe Man, both of whom were unearthed in Denmark during the early 1950's. Though the details of the two finds were different, they were enough alike to hint at an explanation of many of the bog bodies that is both chilling and fascinating.

On May 8, 1950, two men were cutting peat in a spot called Tollund Fen, almost in the center of the Danish peninsula of Jutland. Lifting out a chunk of the dark brown fuel, they were startled to see a human face at the bottom of their excavation. Although the head was almost the same color as the peat, it was so solid and lifelike that the two men jumped to the conclusion that they had come upon a recent murder victim. It would not have been the first time that the bog had been put to such a use.

The peat cutters notified the police in nearby Silkeborg. They expected that the dead man would have to be identified,

Mummified body dating from Denmark's early Iron Age and known as Tollund Man.

his relatives told, and a criminal investigation conducted.

Luckily, the local police had heard that the bog bodies were not always what they seemed. They invited a representative from the local museum to go with them to the scene of the "crime." To the experienced eye of the museum man, and later to the hastily summoned Dr. Glob, it was apparent that the police did not need to waste their time in trying to catch the murderer in this particular case. Like his victim, the "murderer" must have been dead for close to two thousand years. The man whose body lay before them had lived his life during the Iron Age period of Danish history, roughly 400 B.C. to A.D. 400.

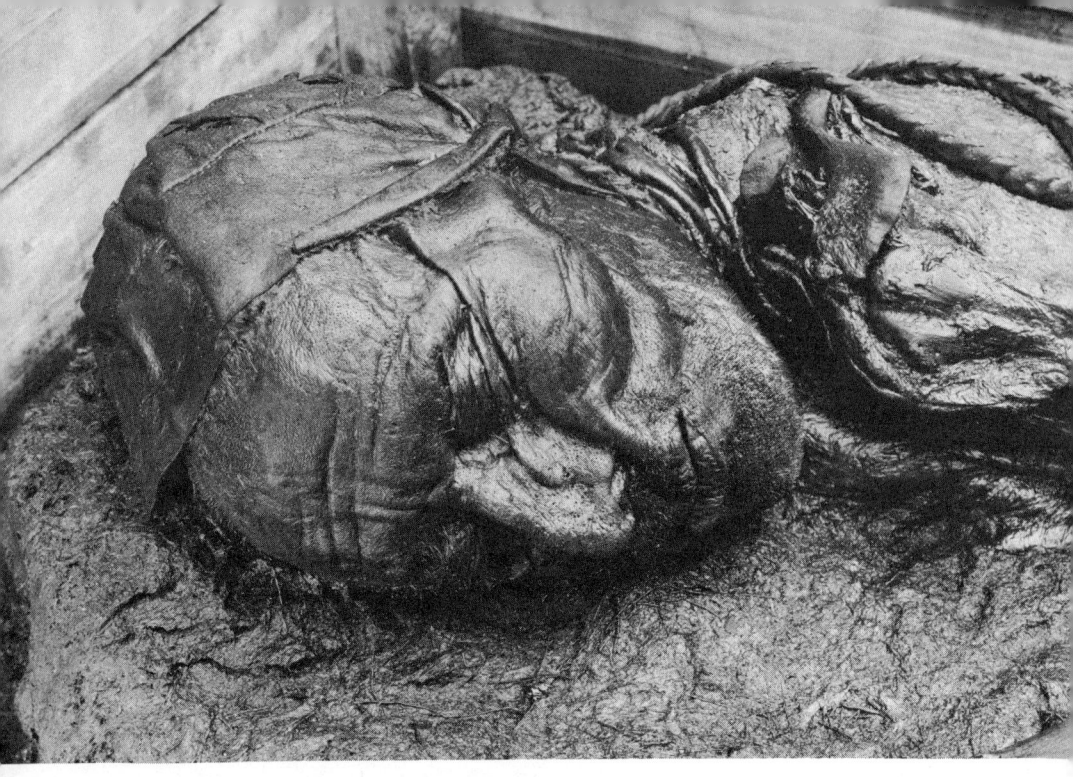

The head of the Tollund Man.

The find was not the first of its kind in the region, by any means, but it was particularly exciting for a number of reasons. The body that began to emerge from the bog under Dr. Glob's direction was one of the best preserved examples ever found. The man lay on his right side with his head toward the west at a point some fifty feet from what had been firm ground before the bog was drained for peat cutting. He had been covered by eight or nine feet of peat, and that alone was enough to show that the body was of a great age.

The first and strongest impression of those who gathered

around the excavation was of the gentle and peaceful expression on the face, as if its owner were about to be awakened from a long, dark sleep. He wore nothing but a pointed skin cap fastened under the chin and a hide belt around his waist. The knees were drawn up in front and the arms partly bent at the elbow, as if for more comfortable sleep.

But the Tollund man had not died in his sleep. One of the workmen moved a block of peat and there, suddenly revealed, was a twisted hide rope drawn in a tight noose round the man's neck and coiled over his shoulder. Could it be murder after all, a murder two thousand years old?

In order to study the body more closely, it was decided to take it to the National Museum in Copenhagen. This was not an easy job, for though the body was in such fine condition it was very fragile and could be damaged badly by jolting or dampness. In the end the mummy and its surrounding block of peat were built into a wooden box, which was then filled with more peat so that the contents could not shift around. The whole crate weighed nearly a ton. It then had to be lifted almost ten feet from the bottom of the bog and carried to the railway by horse-drawn cart, since the surface of the bog was too soft to support the weight of modern lifting equipment. By a sad and curious coincidence, the strain of moving the crate proved too much for one of the workmen, who suffered a fatal heart attack. As Dr. Glob remarked, some might say the bog had claimed a life for a life.

A week later, the Tollund Man reached the laboratories of the Danish National Museum. There, scientists confirmed Dr. Glob's judgment that the body dated from the early Iron Age, a time before Denmark was converted to Christianity, when iron was replacing bronze as the material for tools and weapons. Again, everyone concerned with the find marvelled at the beautiful state of the head. Dr. Glob calls it "the best preserved human head, in fact, to have survived from antiquity in any part of the world." This is probably true, for although some of the Egyptian mummies we saw in Chapter III are nearly as lifelike and fascinating to look at, none are as perfectly preserved from a scientific point of view. In the Tollund Man not only the skin, muscle, and bone are still in an excellent state, but also the hair and even the eyebrows.

Parts of the rest of the body were not in such good condition. On the left side there had been some decay of the chest and shoulder and we can see from the pictures that the body, arms, and legs look like little more than bones covered with skin, although the skin is still astonishingly well-preserved. Only the feet are in a condition nearly as good as that of the head.

Careful examination of the neck led the experts to decide that the Tollund Man had probably met his death by hanging, rather than by simple strangulation. More will be said later about the significance of this conclusion.

Women's clothing from the period of the bog bodies, found in Huldre Fen.

Another interesting fact was discovered through the examination of the internal organs. About twelve hours before he died, the Tollund Man had eaten a rather large meal made up of a mixture of many different kinds of grains and seeds, but no meat.

When the study of the body was completed, the museum authorities had to decide how best to keep it for the future. Now that it was exposed to the air it would probably crumble to dust unless something was done to preserve it. For practical reasons it was decided that only the head could be treated, as the process was a very complicated one. First the head was placed for six months in a water solution of acetic acid and formalin (a modern chemical much used as a preservative). In later stages the solution was changed for one of alcohol in greater and greater concentrations mixed with a solvent called toluol. Eventually the alcohol was replaced by toluol and paraffin, a waxlike substance that is soluble in toluol but not in water. Still later, true wax was substituted. One of the results of all this treatment was that the head became thoroughly saturated with paraffin and wax so it was completely protected from contact with the air.

When the process of study and preservation was finished, the head of the Tollund Man was sent back to the museum in Silkeborg, only a short distance from the place where it had been found.

The area around Tollund had a long history of producing bog bodies, and that history was carried further on April 26, 1952. That day some peat cutters from the village of Grauballe were working in a place called Nebelgard Fen, about eleven miles from Tollund. This time, when they came upon an unmistakable human head in the peat, there was no talk of a recent murder. The men went straight to a local doctor, who was known to be very interested in Iron Age remains. The doctor in turn summoned Dr. Glob, who thus for the second

The bog where Grauballe Man was found.

time in as many years found himself face to face with a complete and undisturbed bog body.

The Grauballe Man lay on his chest in a very old layer of peat. His right arm and leg were bent, one in front of him, one to the rear, while the left arm and leg were relatively straight. He was entirely naked and although the weight of the peat had somewhat flattened and distorted the body and face, it could be seen that his throat had been brutally slashed.

Since the finding of the Tollund Man a new laboratory had been set up to deal with such discoveries. The Grauballe Man was therefore taken to the Museum of Prehistory at Aarhus. Once again, scientists were amazed and delighted at the fine condition of the body. In spite of its twisted position and the weight that had been pressed upon it, the skin and internal organs were just as well-preserved as those of the Tollund Man, and in some cases even better preserved.

The investigation of the body carried out at Aarhus revealed several interesting facts. First, the cause of death was almost certainly the cutting of the throat, and it had been a murder. Such a wound could not have been made by the man himself and could not have been made after death. Furthermore, the Grauballe Man's last meal had been very much like that of the Tollund Man—a mixture of no fewer than sixty-three different kinds of grains and seeds. There were no fruits, no greenstuffs, and in this case, only the slightest trace of meat.

Another feature of the body was that the hands and feet were so well-preserved that the local police were able to take the man's finger- and footprints. They declared that the prints were quite good enough to have been used as evidence in a court case.

Although everything about the Grauballe Man pointed to the fact that he had died during the early Iron Age, as had the Tollund Man and many others of the bog people, it was not as

Grauballe Man after excavation.

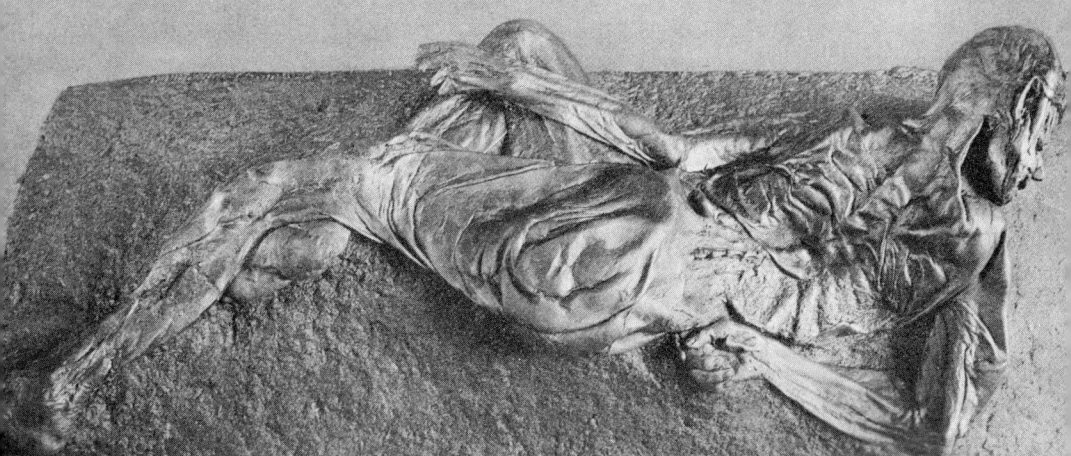

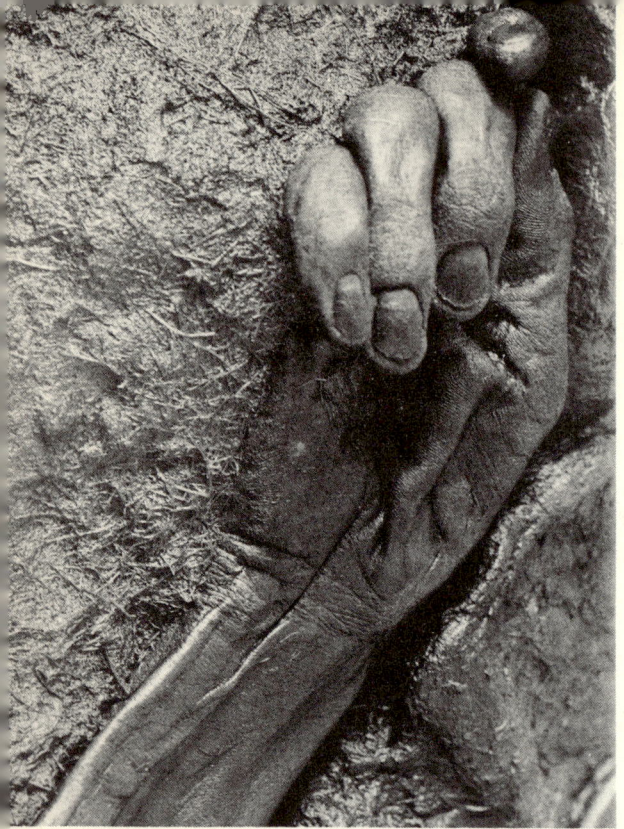

Right hand of Grauballe Man.

Grauballe Man's right foot.

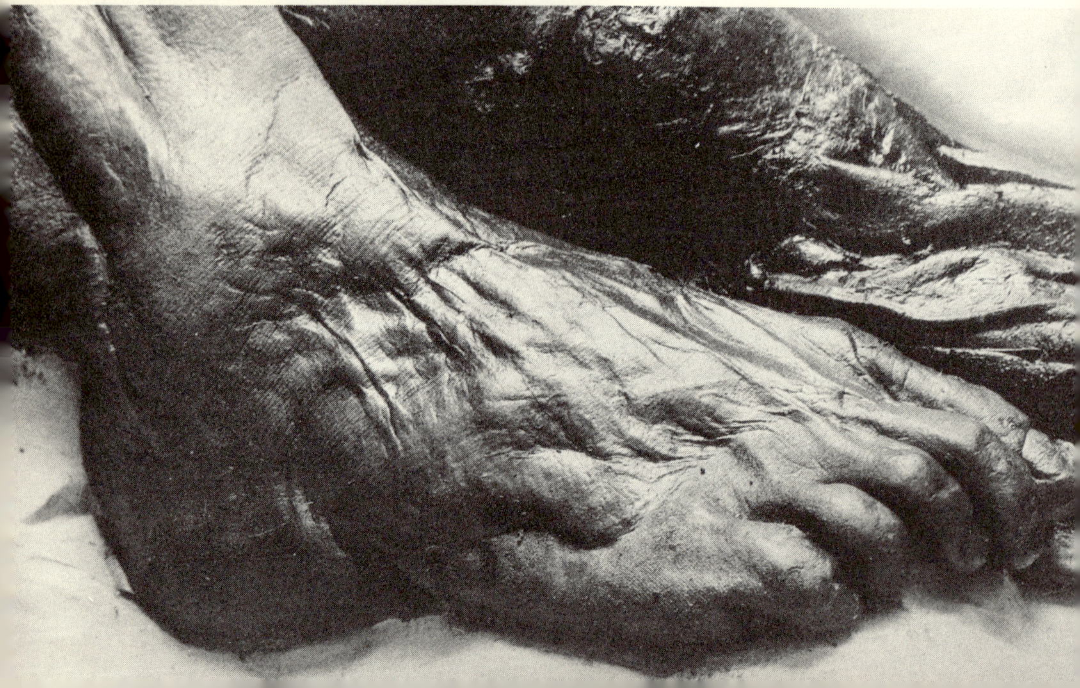

easy to prove the fact as it had been in other cases. Not a single object had been found with him so that the scientists were unable to tell anything from the materials and workmanship of the period. A few years later, however, it became possible to determine the date of the body by other means.

Probably the best known modern method of dating ancient materials is carbon 14 analysis. Since all living things contain a certain amount of radioactive carbon, and since this substance, known as carbon 14, "decays" or changes into another form of carbon at a fixed rate, it is possible to measure the amount of carbon 14 in the tissues of any formerly living organism and judge how many years would have been required for the "decay" of the carbon 14 to give the level found in the specimen. Naturally, the process is not as simple as it sounds, especially since when nations test atomic weapons or permit other kinds of atomic pollution, radiation levels go up all over the world and have to be allowed for in figuring the results. Still, the carbon 14 tests that were run on samples taken from the Grauballe Man gave him a date somewhere between A.D. 210 and 410, which is to say, in the latter part of the early Iron Age.

A second method of dating is called pollen analysis. It is based on the principle that since the world climate has undergone many changes during historical times it should be possible to tell when a certain layer of earth was formed by looking at the pollen grains that are found in it. Every plant species has a different shape for its pollen grains, and since plants will only grow where the environment is right for them, one can tell from the plants that were present what the climate was like and so, within limits, at what time in history those plants were blooming and spreading their pollen. The peat layers of the Danish bogs were filled with the microscopic but still recognizable pollens of the plants that had grown in the surrounding countryside and pollen analysis indicated that the time was somewhere during the first four hundred years A.D. Since there was no contradiction between this and the carbon 14 dating, the scientists felt doubly certain of their opinion that the Grauballe Man had lived in the Iron Age.

It was lucky that the scientific tests gave such plain results. Certain Danish papers had started a rumor that the man found in the fen near Grauballe was not an ancient mummy at all. It was claimed that an old woman of the district had recognized the dead man as a peat cutter named Red Christian who had reputedly disappeared near the bog at some time around 1887. The main argument in favor of this notion was that "everyone knew" that a body couldn't stay in such perfect condition for more than fifteen hundred years. The rumors stopped abruptly with the publication of the carbon 14 test, however. This incident may not reveal much about the history of mummies, but it does serve to show that "common sense" is not always the only way to judge unusual situations.

Although the Tollund Man and the Grauballe Man were probably the most thoroughly studied of the bog people, the riddle of how and why they died in the bog could only be solved in the light of what was known about a variety of other finds. In 1773 a body had been found three feet down in a bog on the Danish Island of Fyn. The man lay on his back with his arms crossed behind him as if they had been bound. His throat had been cut and he was naked except for a sheepskin cap. Several sticks and branches had been laid over the body.

A place called Juthe Fen was the site of a find in 1835. A woman had apparently been taken to the bog, pinned down with a series of stakes, and left to drown. At the time this body was mistakenly identified as that of the legendary Queen Gunhild, who according to tradition had been murdered in a bog in the same general area about a thousand years before. However, all the circumstances of the find point to the fact that "Queen Gunhild" actually belonged to the much earlier pe-

BODIES IN THE BOGS

riod of the Tollund Man and other Iron Age bodies.

In 1946 the body of a naked man was found in Borre Fen. The man had apparently been hung or strangled by a rope that was still around his neck and placed in the bog in a sitting position. At his feet were two sheepskin capes and the body was held in place by birch branches. The man's last meal had been composed of seeds and grains.

On lands owned by an estate called Windeby in the Schleswig section of Germany the body of a young girl was found in 1952. Lying on her back, she was naked except for a woven band that had been used to blindfold her. Apparently she had been drowned, as there was no mark of violence on her body. Several branches and a large stone were found with her. The

The Borre Fen man, discovered in Denmark in 1946. The rope around the neck was probably used to strangle him.

hair on the right side of her head was cut very short, while the left side had apparently been shaved.

Examples of this sort of bog find could fill a great many pages. Perhaps, however, we have listed enough to show what sort of pattern can be seen in them. Any *one* of these bodies, or maybe, over thousands of years, half a dozen, could have come to be in the bogs because of some strange individual circumstance. But that dozens of persons during the same period should have been killed by strangulation or drowning, taken or thrown into the bog naked, and in most cases held down with sticks and stones indicates only one thing. The bog people must have been human sacrifices made to satisfy some power that was believed to inhabit the bog.

If the idea of human sacrifice seems terrible to us now it

Still another body from Borre Fen, this time that of a woman covered with a woolen blanket.

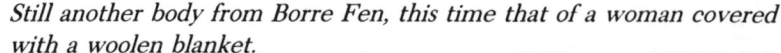

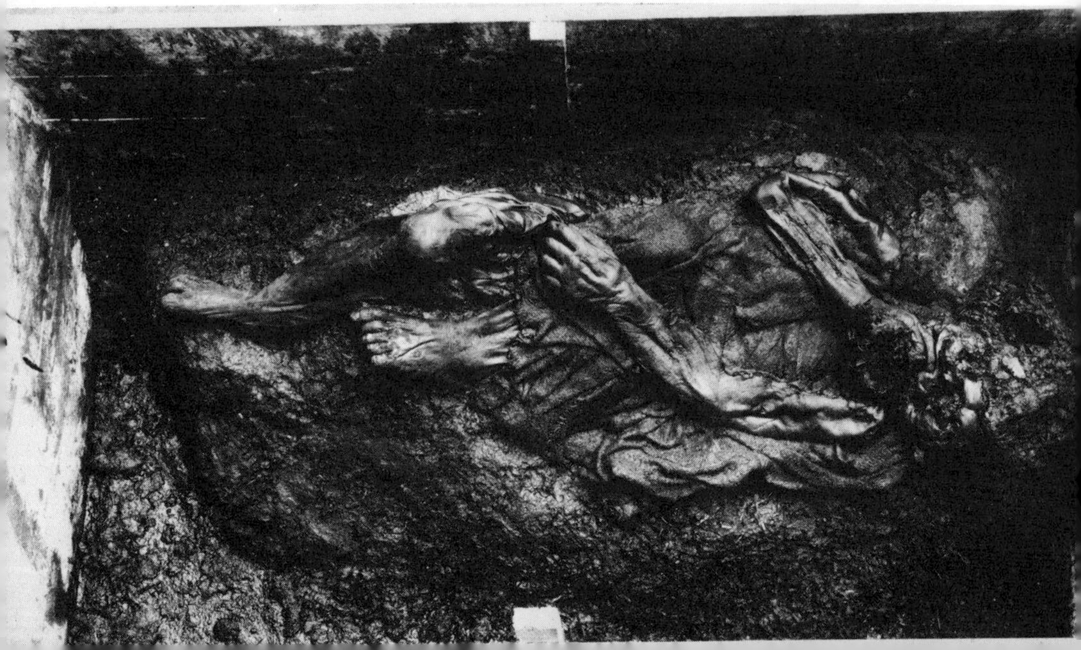

is because we do not see the earth in the same terms as did the people of earlier ages. The Egyptians and Peruvians sought to preserve their bodies for a future life and the effort they expended is a measure of how firmly and vividly they believed their gods controlled both the afterlife and the life of this world. To most ancient peoples, in fact, the gods were thought to be much like human beings, only more powerful. Like human beings, the gods could be selfish, angry, and cruel, as well as generous and loving. The human proverb, "You don't get something for nothing," could have been applied to the dealings of gods with men. Thus since the greatest gift of the gods was of course the food that grew out of the ground it seemed natural that the gift must be paid for in some way. In those days starvation was always a threat, and the people understood very well the idea that food is life. Therefore only human life could pay for the miracle of the yearly harvest. This is an idea that has been found all over the world at various times and, like most of the things human beings do, it is perfectly logical if we understand the reasons behind it.

Once we accept the idea that the Iron Age bog bodies were the victims of sacrifice, many puzzling details become important clues to the way of life during that little-known period. For example, the fact that many of the bog people seem to have made their last meal on a sort of gruel composed of grains and weed seeds almost certainly means that they died during the winter months, when greenstuffs and fruits were not available. When we consider it, this makes sense. When the weather is cold and gray and damp, we often wonder whether spring will ever come. In earlier centuries, it must have seemed to the people that there was some real danger that the warm weather would never return. Midwinter was, therefore, a time when the earth goddess was worshipped with special devotion. The bog people may have been thought of as messengers to the goddess begging her to return to earth and

Carved wooden figure of the goddess Freya, the goddess of the bog, found near Rebild Skovmose in Denmark.

make the grain grow once again. The nature of the victims' last meals may be not only a clue to the time of year but also part of the sacrifice itself. By giving the victim a meal made entirely of grain (with little or no meat, although the people certainly ate meat when they could get it) they may have intended to return to the goddess some of her own bounty.

Incidentally, two British archaeologists once volunteered to sample a batch of gruel made according to the same "recipe" as that eaten by the bog people. In the course of a television broadcast on the subject, the men tried the stuff and decided they would not have cared to live on an Iron Age winter diet. Referring to the suggestion that those chosen for sacrifice may have been criminals, one of the archaeologists declared that a lifetime diet of this gruel would have been punishment enough, no matter what sort of crime the victim had committed. Obviously, though, the archaeologist was not starving at the time.

Another fact about the sacrifices that we can now understand better is the place where they were held. In the soft mud of the bog gifts for the earth goddess sank quickly out of sight, as if they had been taken into the heart of the goddess herself. This probably explains the frequent use of sticks and branches to hold down the corpse. The victim must not only lie on the bog but must be drawn into it. The branches ensured that the bodies would not float to the surface.

It is strange to think that all the painstaking work of the Egyptian mummy-makers was to be surpassed by a people who had exactly the opposite intention—to make the body a part of the earth as quickly and completely as possible.

IX
Crypts, Cranks, and the Kremlin Wall

We have seen that one of the main forces in the worldwide decline of mummification was the influence of the great modern religions. Both Christianity and Islam disapproved strongly of burial practices that gave importance to man's body rather than to his "soul." The Muslim conquerors of Egypt, the Spanish conquerors of Peru and the Canary Islands, and the Christian missionaries to the Aleutians, the South Pacific, and Iron Age Europe all succeeded in imposing their ideas about the treatment of the dead.

It may be surprising, therefore, to note that mummies have been by no means unknown in Europe during the last thousand years. Some of the best and most famous mummies have even been found in monasteries and churches—the very places where one might think they would be least welcome. Another exception to the rule against mummies was sometimes made in the case of great leaders and rulers. One of the earliest examples is probably the embalming of the biblical patriarch Israel, according to Genesis. "... Forty days were

required for it; so many were required for embalming."*
There were probably two reasons for this exceptional action by the ancient Hebrews. First and most obvious, Israel died in Egypt, where his son Joseph had lived for many years. It would be reasonable to follow local custom. Second, it was Israel's last request that he be buried in the tomb prepared for him in the land of Canaan, a long overland journey which an unembalmed corpse would hardly survive.

Another famous historical figure to have undergone some form of mummification was Alexander the Great, at least according to some sources. Alexander died in the midst of his famous campaign to establish an empire in Persia and the Middle East, so *if* his body was actually preserved in some way, it was probably by methods used in Persia at the time, 323 B.C. Several centuries later the Latin writer Cicero wrote that the Persians preserved the dead in wax, while other sources say they used honey. Unfortunately, we know none of the details of the methods used, and although wax would at least have the advantage of keeping the body from contact with airborne bacteria, neither wax nor honey seems likely, by itself, to have been a good long-term preservative.

The next great figure to have the honor of being preserved after death appears to have been the Emperor Charlemagne, who died in A.D. 814. Charlemagne was not only embalmed but dressed in his royal robes and entombed in a sitting position, as if he still occupied the throne. It is interesting to note that, like Israel, who gave his name to the modern nation of Israel, and Alexander, who founded the first great empire ruled from the European continent, Charlemagne also had become a heroic figure to his people. In many respects, the empire he established was the first orderly government of Europe since the fall of Rome three centuries earlier. It may

---

*Gen. 50:3.

be that the idea of the emperor's power had become so important to his people that they felt compelled to believe that, through his preserved body, he was somehow still alive, still "with them" to guide and protect. We have already seen the same attitude applied to the mummified Inca emperors, Tahitian chiefs, and Baganda rulers.

Although their followers may have intended to preserve such great leaders for all time, however, it is not likely that the methods used in Europe during the classical and medieval periods were very successful. Already in the time of Alexander, the art of Egyptian mummy-makers had declined to the point where the most important part of the mummy was its mask or painted portrait, while what is found inside the mummy-case was sometimes little more than a jumbled mass of bones. "The Secrets of Egypt" (which, as we have seen, were not so mysterious after all) had long been forgotten and even learned men believed that the magnificent mummies of three thousand years ago had been made with the aid of magic.

This superstitious belief in the magical nature of mummies was probably partly responsible for the fact that "mummy powder" was a very popular though expensive medicine in medieval times. The English word *mummy* comes from the Arabic word *mum,* which means wax. A similar word in Persian is *mumiya,* meaning pitch or bitumen such as was used by the Egyptians in mummification. Now it happens that bitumen was often used by early Arab physicians, the best in the world at that time, as a treatment for open wounds. It had the advantage of keeping the wound away from air and dirt and may also have acted as a mild antiseptic. At some point a confusion apparently arose as to whether it was supposed to be the mummies made with bitumen (Arabic: *mumiya)* or the bitumen itself that was supposed to be such a powerful medicine. In any case, powdered mummy was for centuries believed to be a sort of wonder drug that could not only cure all ills but give the user long life. This last idea was based on an idea common in early medicine: you will become like anything you swallow. Thus since mummies were known to have lasted thousands of years it was believed that anyone who swallowed mummy powder would also last (that is, live) a long time.

In the years between the fall of Rome and the sixteenth century, mummy was on every physician's list of drugs and many genuine mummies were broken up, powdered, and sold at fabulous prices. When real mummies were not available, quacks were not slow to invent fake powders, which might be anything from charcoal to ground-up animal bones. Some went further and made complete fake mummies, using any dead body they could get their hands on. If the person had died of a contagious disease, this kind of "mummy powder" might actually have made the patient much sicker.

The famous Arab physician Avicenna (980–1037) was fond of prescribing for his patients a potion made with powdered mummy, marjoram, thyme, elder, barley, roses, lentils, jujubes, cumin, caraway, saffron, cassia, parsley, oxymel (vinegar mixed with honey), wine, milk, butter, castor oil, and syrup of mulberries. With so many ingredients, the mixture certainly ought to have been good for something, though it seems unlikely that it was really a cure for abscesses, eruptions, spitting of blood from the lungs, affections of the throat, coughs, palpitations, weakness of the stomach, nausea, disorders of the liver and spleen, ulcers, and poisoning, as Avicenna claimed.

Thus for many centuries in Europe, the word *mummy* was applied to a mysterious and valuable drug as much as to a preserved body.

The Christian Church taught that it was wrong not only to preserve the body but also to study it by cutting it up or in any way treating it with "disrespect." Thus European physicians were forbidden to seek for the knowledge that would enable them to understand and cure the living body as well as preserving the dead one. Under these conditions it is plain that such mummies as are found from the medieval period would have to be natural ones. Although the climate of Europe is generally neither very cold nor very dry, the proper conditions for mummification do occasionally occur.

One of the world's most remarkable groups of natural mummies is in the crypt of the Kievo-Pecherskaya Lavra, a monastery in the Russian city of Kiev. Founded in the eleventh century, the monastery was the home of an active religious community right up until the time of the Russian Revolution. During the eleventh and twelfth centuries it was an important center of culture and scholarship and was especially famous for being the home of the monk Nestor, a man widely revered for his holiness as well as for having written some of the country's earliest chronicles. Nestor died in 1115, or thereabouts, and his mummified body is one of the ninety-six that may now be seen in glass-topped coffins in the deep crypt below the monastery.

The ninety-six mummies of the Kievo-Pecherskaya Lavra date mainly from the time of Nestor and the next few centuries, which probably makes them the oldest surviving European mummies, after the bog bodies. The fact that these bodies became preserved was thought at the time to be a miracle, a tribute to the holy life of the monks. The monastery became a place of pilgrimage for the pious, who traveled long distances to see the wonder of bodies that failed to decay. For more than eight hundred years the monks have lain in their crypt—"dry curled coffee-brown leathered flesh," as one recent visitor described them.* Nowadays, of course, the monastery is a monastery no longer, but a state-run monument of the U.S.S.R. The official guides who conduct visitors through the crypt explain that the "miracle" of preservation is due to the extreme depth and dryness of the crypt and perhaps also to

*Ross Gelbspan, in *The Village Voice* (New York), November 25, 1971.

"something in the air." Soil conditions are such that almost no water or dampness gets through the walls, so that bodies simply dry out when placed there. Another important factor is that the crypt lies so deep that it is below the upper layer of soil in which decay-producing bacteria normally live. Whether these two circumstances alone are enough to account for the mummies is not completely clear. Possibly there are minerals in the soil or in the materials used to build the crypt that, like niter or natron, absorb moisture from the air or otherwise help bring about natural mummification.

Outside the city of Palermo, on the island of Sicily, there is another monastery that is notable for its preserved bodies. Established by monks of the Capuchin Order, the monastery's burial crypt served for years as the last resting place of all the monks who died in the monastery and of certain rich and important citizens of Palermo as well. These mummies are man-made rather than natural ones, however. Travelers who

Some of the mummified monks of Palermo

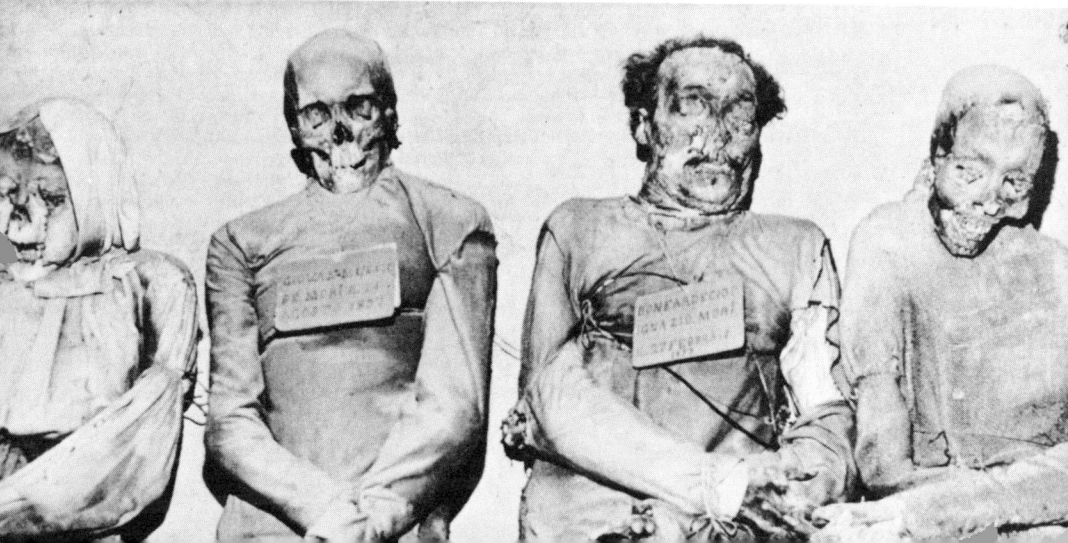

visited the crypts during the last century reported that the bodies were carefully dried before a slow-burning fire. Apparently this process was fairly effective in preserving the general appearance of the body but was far from adequate to give a lifelike appearance. Most observers were either amused or horrified by the weird and twisted expressions of the faces of the Capuchin mummies. One interesting description is that given by a Captain Smyth, who visited the monastery in the 1820's.

> ... Upon descending, it is difficult to express the disgust arising from seeing the human form so degradingly caricatured, in the ridiculous assemblage of distorted mummies that are here hung by the neck in hundreds, with aspects, features, and proportions, so strangely altered by the operation of drying, as hardly to bear a resemblance to human beings. From their curious attitudes, they are rather calculated to excite derision than the awful emotions arising from the sight of 2000 decayed mortals. There are four long galleries with their niches filled, besides many coffins containing noblemen in their court-dress; and among the principal personages is a king of Tunis, who died in 1620. At the end of the great corridor there is an altar, the front of which is formed of human teeth, skulls, etc., and inlaid like mosaic work. There is also an apartment at the end of one of the galleries in which the bodies ... were undergoing the operation of drying, which is effected by means of an oven.*

It would certainly be fascinating if we could know more

---

*Captain Smyth, "Memoir of Sicily and its Islands," cited by T. J. Pettigrew, *A History of Egyptian Mummies*. (London: Longmans, 1834).

about the origins of this form of mummification among the Capuchins, so completely different from the usual burial customs of Christian Europe. However, the island of Sicily has always been known as a place where religious life took unusual and passionate forms. At the time of the monastery's foundation, in the sixteenth century, many devout persons made it a habit to contemplate a *memento mori,* a Latin term for an object that serves as a reminder of death. Possibly the whole display of preserved bodies, and especially the altar made of human skulls and teeth, was intended by the monks as a pious reminder of this sort—a warning to the people that all men must die and that each person should give thought to the state of his soul. Thus if the display in the Capuchin crypt was upsetting and horrifying to visitors, it may have been because that was exactly its purpose. The mummies were intended to show the vanity of earthly life rather than the peace and dignity of death that is expressed by the faces of the pharaohs of Egypt and the monks of Kiev.

For seventeen hundred years it had been forbidden by the Church to tamper with the dead, and exceptions such as those mentioned above were rare. But a change was coming over Europe. The great reevaluation of religious attitudes called the Protestant Reformation and the equally great reevaluation of scientific methods often called the Enlightenment had an almost overwhelming effect on every aspect of life and knowledge. One relatively minor result of these changes was that certain physicians began to study disease by cutting up the bodies of the dead rather than by researching the works of Greek and Roman medical men to find out what treatment was recommended by "the ancients." In the eighteenth century, the new interest in medical research quickly led to a search for new methods of preserving bodies. A physician would not want the organs he was dissecting to decay before he had finished examining them, especially if he wanted to keep his specimens for discussion with students or other researchers. As a result, many new techniques were tested, using such substances as turpentine, oil of rosemary, tar, plaster of paris, and alcohol. The principal purpose was not, of course, mummification of the whole body, but rather a temporary preservation for study or more permanent preservation of individual organs. Nevertheless, the methods developed in this century were certainly good enough to have been used for complete mummification, as is proved by the remarkable tale of "The Dear Departed."

In 1775, in England, there lived a physician named Martin Van Butchell. Dr. Van Butchell had some very odd ideas about the practice of medicine and also about other matters; he was, in short, both a quack and a nut. But Dr. Van Butchell was lucky in one respect at least. He had a wealthy wife, whose money had supported him through many professional ups and downs. Unfortunately, Mrs. Van Butchell chose this time to die, leaving her husband with a very difficult problem. It seems that Mrs. Van Butchell's family, not being too enthusiastic about their son-in-law, had made legal arrangements so that he should control her money only, in the words of the document, "as long as she was above ground."

Now Dr. Van Butchell had a brilliant, if strange, idea. His "dear departed" wife should simply stay above ground forever. He commissioned Dr. William Hunter, the country's most famous anatomist and later president of the Royal Academy of Arts, to embalm the body. Van Butchell may have been a quack himself, but he knew how to hire the best. Dr. Hunter's principal technique was to inject a solution of two kinds of turpentine, oil of rosemary, oil of lavender, and vermilion into the blood vessels. He also washed all the internal organs in camphorated spirits of wine and filled all the body cavities with a powder of camphor, resin, and niter. The body was then rubbed with oils of rosemary and lavender and dried on a bed of plaster. By this treatment, he produced a splendidly well-preserved and lifelike mummy. Thereafter the delighted widower kept his wife's mummy in the parlor, visible proof that the poor lady was still "above ground."

Word of "The Dear Departed" quickly got about, and soon the Van Butchell house began to receive a steady stream of curious visitors. The doctor was apparently only too happy to show them what they wanted to see, but eventually he was forced to limit visiting hours—"daily from 9 to 1, closed Sunday." But the custom came to an end when the mummy was removed from the house due to the protests of Dr. Van Butchell's second wife, who perhaps did not like having to dust her predecessor. In any case, "The Dear Departed" found its way to the museum of the Royal College of Surgeons, where it was destroyed during the bombing of London in 1941.

As we have seen, most mummies have been made for religious purposes, a few for scientific or political reasons. "The Dear Departed" is perhaps the only example of a mummy made for financial reasons, while the next case of mummification we shall look at came about for reasons that can only be called social.

Jeremy Bentham (1748-1832) was an English philosopher whose many interests included law, morals, chemistry, botany, and music. His greatest fame, however, rests on his development of Utilitarianism. This doctrine taught that the only sound basis for making political, economic, personal, or any other kind of decision was to consider which course of action would bring about the greatest good of the greatest number of people. Without going into the complexities of the subject, we may still see that such a philosophy could only be held by someone who took a very practical view of life. A follower of Utilitarianism would be bound to ignore the influences of emotion, faith, or tradition, and to do only those things that he or she thought most useful to the world.

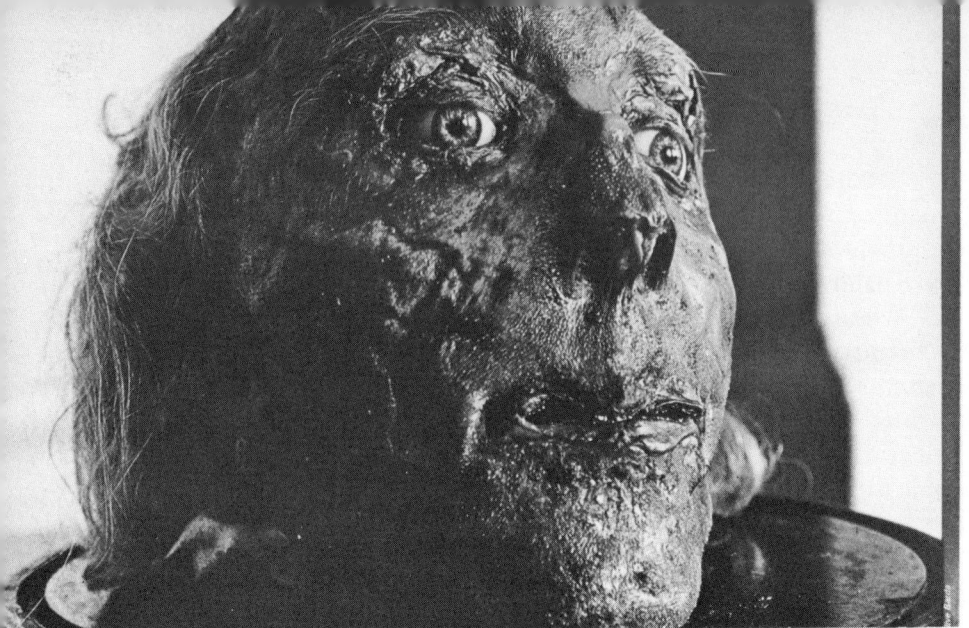

The head of Jeremy Bentham, mummified according to the terms of his will

There is nothing surprising in the fact that Jeremy Bentham should have tried to live his life according to the principles of his own teaching. That he should apply those principles to his death is a little less predictable, but serves to show the strength of his conviction. Bentham's will directed that his body should be dissected for a group of students as illustration of a lecture on human anatomy. After the lecture, the body (but not the head) was to be reduced to a skeleton and strung together with wire. The head, meanwhile, was to be carefully preserved and equipped with glass eyes. Finally the skeleton, topped by the preserved head, was to be dressed in Bentham's clothes and brought out to attend each meeting of the Utilitarian Society.

CRYPTS, CRANKS, AND THE KREMLIN WALL

Bentham's instructions were carried out to the letter, according to methods he had worked out with the help of his friend Thomas Southwood Smith. The remains of Jeremy Bentham are now owned by London's University College and are still brought out for meetings of Utilitarians, although it was found necessary some years ago to replace the original head with a wax copy. It is interesting that, although the use of the body for an anatomy demonstration fitted in very well with Utilitarian ideas, Bentham's wish to go on attending the lively debates of his fellow Utilitarians seems to have been more sentimental than practical. He simply didn't want to miss anything.

In the past two centuries the Americas have been the scene of some remarkable mummifications. One bizarre accident was the preservation of a man named Wilhelm Von Ellenbogen, who in 1792 died of yellow fever and was buried in a waterside grave near Philadelphia. The marshy ground of the burial site happened to be highly alkaline, so that there was a chemical reaction in the fatty tissues of the body very similar to that which occurs in the making of soap. Among its other qualities, soap is harder and slower to decay than unalkalized fats, so that when the Soap Man was accidentally dug up several decades later, he was remarkably well mummified by a method we have not met with before.

No matter how strange the method of mummification, most mummies have the common history of having been buried and later dug up. Not so, however, in a grisly anecdote from Laurinberg, North Carolina. In 1911 a circus musician named Frinnizzee Concippio came through the little town with a traveling show. Somehow, Concippio and another performer got into a fight over a woman in which the musician was killed. (A jury later ruled that the killing was done in self-defense.) Concippio's body was taken to the town undertaker for burial and a man who identified himself as the victim's father came to identify the body. The old man then gave the undertaker fifty dollars as part payment for the funeral service and promised to come back as soon as he had raised the rest of the money. However, days passed, the circus left town, and Mr. Concippio's father failed to return. At first the undertaker did what he could to preserve the body for the delayed funeral, using the usual embalming fluids. Later, still patient but pressed for space, he tied a rope around the body and hung it from the wall of the embalming room, where it gradually dried out. And there, according to a newspaper story of August, 1962, it still hangs—an accidental mummy if ever there was one.

Although the fact of natural mummification will, of course, be with us whenever conditions are favorable, one might be tempted to say that the custom of artificial mummification had nearly disappeared from the modern world. It is true that there is probably no group of people who still mummify their dead as a matter of course, unless in some remote area of Southeast Asia, Australia, or the South Pacific. Even the Jivaros, under pressure from the local government, have largely given up the making of new *tsantsas,* although the old trophies are still proudly displayed. Yet if one looks closely at the world today, it becomes clear that something of the same impulse that once led to the making of mummies is still at work, perhaps growing even stronger, among the people in general, and that in some special cases the custom of preserving dead leaders is also still with us.

In the last few years several books and articles have been written about the change that has come over funeral customs in the United States, and to a lesser extent in Europe as well. Not only the "cost of dying" has greatly increased, but also the concern for the actual condition of preservation of the dead body. In the eighteenth and early nineteenth centuries, the plain pine coffin and the carved tombstone or wooden marker were about the only equipment needed for a funeral. Buried in the damp earth, both box and body soon decayed—how soon depended on soil and weather conditions. In this way the phrase from the widely used funeral service from the Book of Common Prayer became a reality—"earth to earth, ashes to ashes, dust to dust." Most religions taught that only the soul was immortal, while the dead body was simply a shell which was made of the same basic materials as all earth and which should be allowed to go back to the earth. Recently, however, the manufacturers of coffins and the professional people who make arrangements for funerals have begun to claim that their products and procedures can slow down, if not do away with, the natural processes of decay.

Much of this development has been made possible by modern knowledge of chemistry. There are many chemicals, of which formalin is only the best known, that are very effective in preserving, or "pickling," animal tissue for quite long periods. Formalin and similar substances work by "denaturing," or changing the structure of the protein molecules that make up animal tissue. Denatured protein is not broken down by the natural enzymes. Most biology courses offer students a chance to examine laboratory specimens that have been preserved in this way. The technique can also be used on the human body, of course, although it becomes much more complicated when the purpose is to produce a lifelike impression rather than a laboratory specimen. Part of the reason for the increased use of embalming is the increased popularity of "viewing the body." In earlier times the coffin was usually kept closed before and during the funeral ceremony, but more and more families have recently been choosing to keep the coffin open, as if to give the impression that the dead person was still present "in the body" instead of "in the spirit." Now, it is obvious that if a body is going to be on view for any length of time, certain things will have to be done to it in order to hide any signs of decay or other natural but upsetting changes that take place after death. The well-known stiffening of the muscles called *rigor mortis*, for example, sometimes causes the face and body to assume quite unnatural expressions or positions. Thus, if viewing the body is the custom, a certain amount of embalming is inevitable.

Strangely enough, however, no one seems to be able to say why this change in funeral customs has come about. Funeral directors and coffin salesmen generally say they have offered the public only what it demanded—bigger, more expensive "caskets" enclosed in concrete or metal vaults and guaranteed to last almost forever, plus elaborate, more expensive chemical treatment of the body "in order to spare the relatives the pain of knowing the body has decayed." On the other hand, some writers have suggested that the funeral industry has itself created the demand for more thoroughly preserved bodies because the more expensive and elaborate the funeral the greater their profits. The idea is that the dead person's relatives will usually agree that they want "only the best" and leave it up to the funeral director to show them what "the best" is. In spite of the advertised claims, the usual modern embalming technique probably does not preserve the body for more than a few months, except in special circumstances.

The odd thing is that none of the major religions has changed its teachings about the relative unimportance of the dead body, but few have really objected to the new attitudes. No doubt there would be more protest if actual complete mummification were to become popular. Considering what we now know about ancient methods, coupled with modern developments such as quick-freezing and the use of embalming fluids made with arsenic, alcohol, and various alkalis, it is probably not impossible for the modern world to adopt mummification if enough people wish to do so. Such a change would of course raise an enormous space problem on a planet that no longer has enough room for the living. It might also make us think again about what it is that makes man want to preserve his body in the first place. If we do not mummify our dead in order to have the advice of great leaders, as did the Polynesians, to prove their holiness, as did the Russian monks, to show the continuing power of the emperors, as did the Incas, to provide a home for the spirit, as did the Egyptians, to arouse the fear of divine judgment, as did the monks of Palermo, or even to destroy the evil magic of our enemies, as did the Jivaros—then is it simply the ancient fear of death that has made some modern individuals try to preserve their bodies?

We have already mentioned above that one modern method of keeping dead bodies for lengthy periods might be freezing. An astonishing notion derived from this idea is the preservation of the living, or even the preservation of the dead —so that they may live again. Many animals that live in cold climates survive by hibernating, that is, by lowering their body temperatures and entering a deep and lasting sleeplike state until warmer weather replaces the harsh winter. Now modern medical techniques have enabled physicians to create similar states in animals and even human beings for rather long periods of time. Among other effects, the heartbeat is slowed to such an extent that the patient could not survive if his body were at a normal temperature.

These developments have led some researchers to wonder whether it might not in the future be possible for human beings to enter the state of "hibernation," "suspended animation," or "cryonic sleep" (as it is variously called), more or less at will. A person who was dissatisfied with his or her present life might then be able to be "put away" for any length of time desired, until, for example, a cure had been found for some fatal disease that afflicted him. Even more fascinating, from the point of view of mummification, is the idea that a person who had been declared dead by medical science might be frozen and then brought back to life. Already this possibility has been taken beyond the stage of mere pipe dreams. In 1967 Dr. James H. Bedford of California, a retired professor of psychology, died of cancer. Immediately upon Dr. Bedford's death, and according to the terms of his will, physicians went to work to keep his heart beating artificially. Then the temperature of the body was lowered to eight degrees Centigrade and most of the blood was replaced by a very long-lasting solvent. Next the temperature was lowered to minus seventy-nine degrees, and the body was sent by air to Phoenix, Arizona, where it was stored, and is still in storage, at the very low temperature of minus one hundred ninety degrees Centigrade. Dr. Bedford's will had provided money for all these processes and also for the continued maintenance of his body (at a cost of about $280 a year). As a member of the Cryonics Society of California, one of several groups devoted to the preservation of bodies at low temperatures, he had become convinced that it would one day be possible to revive him, even though he had been pronounced dead before being frozen. The treatment given the body was carefully designed to do the least possible damage to its cells and although most physicians hold out small hope that Dr. Bedford can ever be successfully revived, it does seem at least conceivable that others who have been frozen by more advanced methods may one day be restored to life. Several foundations and research centers are pursuing the possibility, among them the Bedford Foundation for Cryobiological Research, endowed with $200,000 by the psychologist's will.

If the revival of the dead should become possible in some such way as this, it would raise several very complicated questions about the definition of mummies and even of death itself. Can a cryonically frozen body be called a mummy, and if so, are mummies always dead? If a being is dead now, according to all our definitions, but may become living again in the future, how can we be sure what we mean by "dead"? Can we even admit the possibility that by "mummifying" our dead now, like the Egyptians and others, we might achieve actual immortality, the conquest of death, in the future?

It is not really very likely that we shall see a widespread return to mummification in the Western world. However, there is one very well-known example of mummification in the twentieth century, although it is seldom called by that name. Yet, in terms of all we have seen and heard of mummies, the body of Lenin that is on public view in its tomb near the wall of Moscow's Kremlin is certainly a mummy. Vladimir Ilyich Lenin (1870–1924) is often described as the founder of Soviet Russia. His work and writings had the most important possible role in shaping the Communist government of Russia after the Revolution. Lenin's personal leadership and example were as widely known and admired as his writings. Like other such national figures, from George Washington to Hitler, Lenin came to be a *symbol* of certain ideas and historical events. When he died it was not surprising that he should have been mourned as a national hero. But the Soviet government did more. Lenin's body was placed in a specially built crypt, through which tens of thousands of visitors still continue to file each year. On national holidays the line of ordinary Russian citizens waiting to pay their respects to the corpse is often many blocks long. It is a saying in the modern U.S.S.R. that "Yesterday, today, and tomorrow, Lenin is always with us." The presence of his apparently perfectly preserved body in the tomb obviously helps to strengthen that sort of belief in the eternal rightness and importance of his teaching.

The fact that Russia has a tradition of revering the "miraculously" preserved bodies of holy men such as the monks in the Kievo-Pecherskaya Lavra helps to explain why the tomb of Lenin is such an important place in the Soviet Union today. It also helps explain why the Soviet government does not give out information about the methods used to pre-

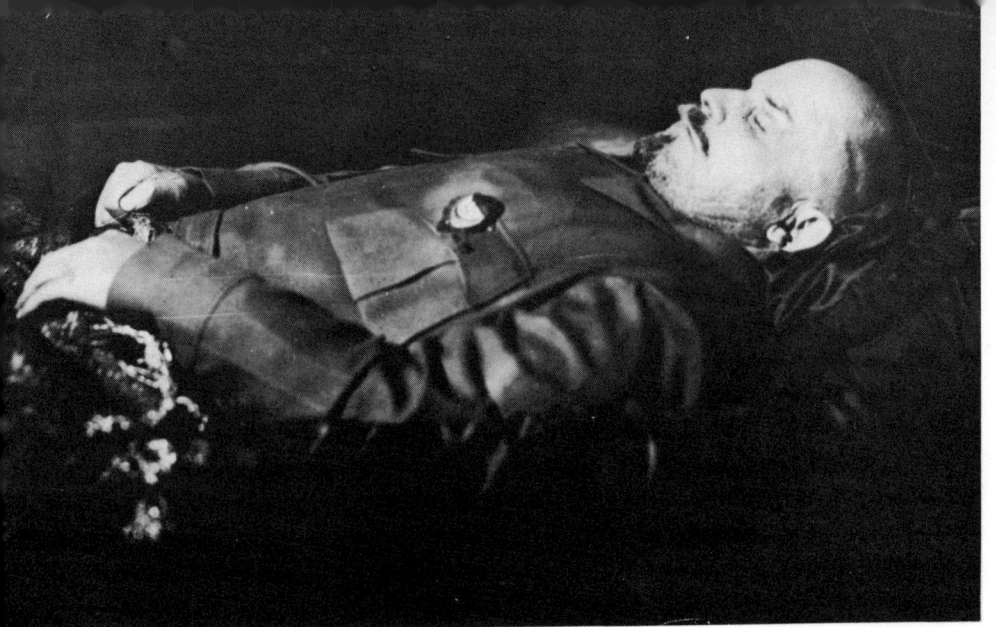

The body of V. I. Lenin as it looks today, lying in the marble mausoleum erected for it on Red Square, Moscow

serve Lenin's body, although it is obvious that a great deal of trouble must have been taken. Partly as a result of this official silence, no doubt, a rumor has recently been reported from Moscow, suggesting that the actual body had to be replaced with a wax model after sewers overflowed into the tomb. Whether or not this suspicion is the truth, the important point is that millions of Russians believe that they are in some sense closer to the spirit of Lenin because his body is still among them. Merely because we have moved into the twentieth century, we have not lost our interest in bodies, our fascination with death, or our feeling that somehow the body *is* the person.

Suggestions for Further Reading

The Book of the Dead, translated and with an introduction by E. A. Wallis Budge, University Books, 1960.
Carter, Howard, *The Tomb of Tut-ankh-Amen,* 3 volumes, Cassell, 1933.
Digby, Bassett, *The Mammoth and Mammoth-Hunting in North-East Siberia,* H., F., & G. Witherby, 1926.
Glob, P. V., *The Bog People,* Cornell University Press, 1969.
Mason, J. Alden, *The Ancient Civilizations of Peru,* Penguin, 1957.
McCracken, Harold, *God's Frozen Children,* Doubleday, 1930.
Mitford, Jessica, *The American Way of Death,* Simon & Schuster, 1963.
Pettigrew, Thomas Joseph, *A History of Egyptian Mummies,* Longmans, 1834.
Smith, Grafton Elliot, *The Migrations of Early Culture,* Manchester University Press, 1929.

Index

Aarhuś, 126, 127
aborigines, 109, 115
Adams, M. F., 22, 23
Africa, 21, 117
afterlife, 15, 16, 17, 34, 37, 44, 45, 47, 53, 111, 115, 133
Alaska, 12, 72-79, 114
Aleutian Islands, 72, 74, 76, 78, 85, 114, 136
Alexander the Great, 137, 138
Amazon River, 83, 86, 105
Americans, native, 72, 80-83
Ancón, 93-100
Andes, 83, 91
animal mummies, 17-18, 36-37, 99-100
animals, sacred, 37-38
Asia, 18, 27, 30, 114, 148
Atlantis, 112
Australia, 108-111, 114, 148
Avicenna, 139

Baganda, 112-113, 117
Bedford, Dr. James H., 152
Bentham, Jeremy, 145-147
Beresovska mammoth, 23-32
Blumenbach, Johann, 21
bog bodies, 118-135, 140
Bolivia, 87
Book of the Dead, 47, 70, 72
Borneo, 111
Borre Fen, 131
British Museum, 71
burial chamber, 60-63, 66, 74
burial practices, 102, 136; African, 112-113; Aleutian Island, 74-77, 85-86; American Indian, 80-82; Australian, 108-110; Canary Islands, 117; Egyptian, 34; European, 148-150; Indonesian, 110; Neanderthal, 16; New Guinea, 110; New Zealand, 106-107; Peruvian, 89-93, 96-101; Polynesian, 105-106; U.S., 148-150

INDEX 157

Canary Islands, 12, 111, 116, 117, 136
Capuchin Order, mummies of, 141, 142, 143
carbon 14, 129, 130
Carnarvon, Lord, 55-69
Carter, Howard, 55-70
caves, mummy, 12, 73, 74, 112, 114
cemetery. *See* necropolis
Charlemagne, Emperor, 137
chemical preservatives. *See* preservatives
Chile, 87, 104
China, 19, 20, 114
Christianity, 139, 143; opposition to mummification in, 44, 88, 89, 92, 123, 136, 143
chullpas, 92
Cicero, 137
climate, effect of, 28, 34, 72, 75, 106, 110, 114, 129
coffin, 34, 44, 58, 64, 65, 108, 117, 140, 148, 149, 150
Concippio, Frinnizzee, 147-148
Cook, Captain, 105
Cook Islands, 108
Copper Man, 104
Cro-Magnon man, 112
cryonics, 151-152
Cryonics Society of California, 152
Curse of the Pharaohs, 67-71
Cuvier, Baron, 26, 27, 28
Cuzco, 87

"Dear Departed," The, 144-145
death, attitudes toward, 15-17, 34, 37, 44-47, 89, 90, 96, 98, 99, 115, 133, 143, 149, 150, 152, 153, 154
Denmark, 12, 118-135
dinosaurs, 18, 28

Ecuador, 87
Egypt, 12, 33-51, 52-71, 85, 87, 89, 99, 110, 113, 115, 116, 117, 124, 133, 135, 136, 137, 138, 143, 151, 153
Egyptian: burial customs, 100, 103, 104; mummies, 12, 33-51, 66-67; mummy cases, 108; mummy-makers, 12; pharaohs, 46, 53, 54, 64, 67, 68, 70
embalming. *See* mummification, methods of
Enlightenment, the (historical period), 143
Europe, 18, 23, 26-27, 30, 94, 112, 137, 138, 143

Florida, 82
Ft. Caspar, Wyoming, 81
funeral customs. *See* burial practices
Fyn, 130
fyn shu, 20

Germany, 119, 131
glaciers, 30-32
Glob, Dr. P. V., 120-125
gods, 38, 62, 87, 100, 133
goddess, earth, 133-135
Grauballe Man, 120, 125-130
grave. *See* tomb
Great Britain, 119
Guanches, 111-112, 115, 116, 117
Gunhild, Queen, 130

Hall, Captain Basil, 102-103
Hannibal, 21
headhunters, 83
head-shrinking, 83-86
Hebrews, ancient, 136-137
Hennig, Captain E., 73
Herodotus, 36, 37, 38, 51
Hertz, Dr. Otto, 24, 25, 30
Heyerdahl, Thor, 116
hibernation, 151
hieroglyphics, 44
Hippocrates, 51
Holland, 119
Hongi, Hare, 107
huaoqui, 91
huito, 84, 86
human sacrifice, 132, 133-135
Hunter, Dr. William, 144

158 INDEX

Ice Age, 17, 19, 27, 28, 30, 32
Ides, Isbrant, 20
immortality. *See* afterlife
Incas, 72, 87-91, 103-104, 138, 151
India, 21, 114
Indigirca River, 21
Indonesia, 110, 111, 114
internal organs. *See* viscera
Iron Age (European), 121, 123, 127, 129, 131, 133, 134, 136
Islam, 44, 136
Island of the Four Mountains, 73-74, 77
Israel, 136-137
Italy (Palermo), 140-143

Japan, 114
Jivaros, 83-86, 105, 148, 151
Juthe Fen, 130
Jutland, 120

Kagamil Island, 72, 77
Kauava, 108
Kentucky, 79-80, 82, 114
Kiev, 140, 143
Kievo-Pecherskaya Lavra Monastery, 140, 153
Kingdom of the Dead, 37, 47, 89
Kremlin, 153

Lamut tribe, 23
Lemaistre mummy, 109-110
Lena River, 22, 23
Lenin, Vladimir Ilyich, 153-154
Lisle, James, 81
Logan, Josias, 20

magic, 16, 44, 47, 49, 50, 62, 67, 86, 106, 138
mammoth, woolly, 17, 18-32, 73; discovery of, 20-24; ivory of, 19, 20, 22, 23, 26
Mammoth Cave, Kentucky, 79-80, 114
Mangaia, 108
Maoris, 106-108, 110
Maranon River, 83
mastabas, 52

McClure's Magazine, 73
McCracken, Harold, 73-77, 81
medicine: mummification and, 49, 50, 51, 139, 143; use of mummies in, 138-139
Metropolitan Museum of Art, 59
Middle Ages, 20, 139-140
mummies: animal, 17-18, 37, 99; artificial, 12, 17, 33, 34, 148; definition of, 11; natural, 12, 16, 17, 33, 140, 147-148
mummification, methods of, 11, 12, 144; Africa, 112-113; Alaska, 76-77; ancient, 136-137; Canary Islands, 115-117; Denmark, 118-135; Inca, 89; Jivaro, 83-85; modern, 150-154; Neanderthal, 16, 138; Palermo, 141-142; Peru, 102-104; U.S., 80-82; U.S.S.R., 140-141; Van Butchell, 144
mummy bundles, 96, 114
"Mummy 49," 101
mummy powder, 138-139
Museum of Prehistory, Aarhus, 126
Muslim conquest of Egypt, 136

National Museum, Copenhagen, 123
Neanderthal Man, 16
Nebelgard Fen, 125
necropolis, 45, 91-94
Nestor, 140
New Guinea, 109-111, 115-116
New Zealand, 12, 106-107
North Africa, 111, 116
North America, 18, 30, 72-82, 110, 113

Pacific Islands, 105-117, 136, 148
Palermo, 141-143, 151
panaca, 90
Papuans, 110, 115-116
Paracus, 100-101
Persia, 137
Peru, 12, 87-104, 110, 114, 115, 133, 136
Peter the Great, 20
Pizarro, 87, 91
pollen analysis, 129
Polynesia, 105, 106, 108, 110, 114, 115, 151

Polynesian Society, 107; *Journal,* 107
portrait mask, 44
preservatives (used in mummification), 11, 12, 16, 36, 38, 39, 41, 44, 66, 76, 80, 81, 82, 84, 86, 106, 107, 119, 125, 137, 138, 141, 143, 144, 149
Prince William Sound, 77
Protestant Reformation, 143
pyramids, 12, 52

"racial old age," 30
Ramses IV, 56
religion, influence of, on mummification, 99, 100, 150
revival of the dead, 151, 152
rigor mortis, 150
Russia. *See* U.S.S.R.
Russian Academy of Sciences, 23
Russian Orthodox Church, 78
Russian Revolution, 140, 153

sacred head, 106
sarcophagus, 58, 61, 62, 63, 64
Scandinavia, 119
scarab, 47
Schumakhof, Ossip, 22, 23
Siberia, 18-32
Sicily, 141, 143
Silkeborg, 120, 125
Smith, Thomas Southwood, 147
Smithsonian Institution, 73
Smyth, Captain, 142
Soap Man, 147
soul, 15, 50
South America, 82-104, 114, 115, 148
Spanish conquest of Peru, 87-89, 91, 94, 103, 115, 136
spirit, 15, 16, 17, 93, 96, 98, 106, 110, 149, 151
spirit heads, 96
Sredne-Kolymsk, 24
Steindorff, Georg, 69-70
Sumatra, 111
superstitious beliefs concerning mummies, 138

suspended animation, 151

tabus, 106
Tahiti, 105-106, 138
Tartars, 20
Tollund Fen, 120
Tollund Man, 120-125, 126, 131
tomb, 12, 52, 53, 55, 114; furnishings of, 45, 46, 53, 55-71, 76, 89-94, 92-100, 98-101
tomb-robbing, 47, 48, 49, 52, 53, 54, 55, 58, 59, 62, 66, 68, 94
Torres Strait, 109
tree burial, 107, 110
tree-worship, 110
tsantsa, 85, 86, 148
Tungus, 22, 23
Tut-ankh-Amen, King, 55-71

Uganda, 112-113
University of Chicago, 59
U.S.A., 79-82, 147-148
ushabti, 46, 47, 91
U.S.S.R., 21-30, 140-141, 153-154
Utilitarianism, 145, 147

Valley of the Kings, 53, 55, 62
Van Butchell, Dr. Martin, 144
Velikovsky, Immanuel, 28-29
Viracocha, 91
Virginia, 82
viscera, 35, 36, 40, 41, 50, 76, 80, 103, 106, 109, 113, 125

wambo, 85
Windeby girl, mummy, 131
Wyoming, 81

Zoological Museum of Leningrad, 26

About the Author

As a child, Georgess McHargue had an interesting existence divided between sidewalk hopscotch in New York City and galloping about southwestern Montana in the summers. She read a great deal and began writing poetry, an art she continues to pursue.

After receiving her degree at Radcliffe, Ms. McHargue entered the publishing field and before long began writing her own books. Her deep interests in archaeology, folklore, and the occult often find their way into her books, in titles such as THE BEASTS OF NEVER, THE IMPOSSIBLE PEOPLE, and FACTS, FRAUDS & PHANTASMS. She has also written books for younger readers.

Ms. McHargue lives in New York City with a cat who adopted her.